PILGRIMAGES

PILGRIMAGES

Richard Barber

THE BOYDELL PRESS

First published 1991 by the Boydell Press, Woodbridge

First published in paperback 1997
Reprinted 1998

ISBN 0 85115 519 7 hardback
ISBN 0 85115 471 9 paperback

The Boydell Press is an imprint of Boydell & Brewer Ltd
PO Box 9, Woodbridge, Suffolk IP12 3DF, UK
and of Boydell & Brewer Inc.
PO Box 41026, Rochester NY 14604–4126, USA

A catalogue record for this book is available
from the British Library

Library of Congress Catalog Card Number: 91–3366

This publication is printed on acid free paper

Printed in Great Britain by
Athenæum Press Ltd, Gateshead, Tyne & Wear

Contents

Preface

A short book on a large subject always needs a brief note by way of preface, to set out the ground on which the author hopes to meet his reader. This is not a religious book, and it does not to claim to be inspired by any particular viewpoint. Rather, it is a historian's view of a worldwide phenomenon, an attempt to bring together the material on an aspect of religion that is one of the great common experiences of mankind, but one which has not been documented except within the confines of each religion. I know of only one book which attempts the same kind of survey as the present volume (*Les chemins de Dieu* by Jean Chélini and Henry Branthomme) and I am conscious that I have been rash in attempting to cover such a vast subject. The sin will be compounded, for the devout at least, because I cannot claim to have shared the pilgrim's experience, even if I have travelled on some of their roads. I can only humbly offer this as a view from outside, but one which I hope will encourage and challenge others to take up the themes outlined in this essay.

I am grateful to Justin Knowles, who originally suggested the subject, with a rather different approach in mind, and to Derek and Elisabeth Brewer, fellow-travellers on the road to Compostela a decade ago, who kindly read the text and made many useful comments.

Richard Barber

Introduction

Pilgrimage, the journey to a distant sacred goal, is found in all the great religions of the world. It is a journey both outwards, to new, strange, dangerous places, and inwards, to spiritual improvement, whether through increased self-knowledge or through the braving of physical dangers. It can also encompass penance for past sins and the search for physical benefits through the medium of a god or saint, either in the form of the resolution of mundane problems or the cure of a physical ailment. At one extreme, the pilgrim may pursue spiritual ecstasy in seeking out the place where the founder of his or her religion once lived and taught; at the other he or she may look for a miracle that offers purely physical benefits.

What follows is a brief survey of the great pilgrimage traditions. In a short book such as this, we can only touch on the vast range of pilgrim experience, mainly in terms of its outward manifestations, let alone explore its multifarious spiritual dimensions. To carry out a full comparison of the pilgrimage systems of the major religions would be a formidable task, and it is one which has never yet been attempted. All we can do within the scope of the present survey is to outline the history and nature of the different ideas and rites of pilgrimage, and to bring together by way of conclusion some of the themes which emerge in the process. These reveal a surprising consistency of practice, often down to small details, among pilgrims of widely differing beliefs and times.

Because pilgrimage has always been deeply attached to

1

place, the figure of the pilgrim was never a familiar sight except to those who lived on the roads which led to the sacred sites. Yet throughout the world the idea of pilgrimage is understood and accepted as a natural activity. Today the pilgrims are no longer so easily identified by distinctive garb; they are no longer the only travellers who are not royal officials or traders. Instead, they move invisibly in huge numbers among the tourists of today, indistinguishable from them except in purpose. The pilgrimage to Mecca can attract almost two million travellers a year, while the vast tide of men and women that flows to the Ganges at Prayaga for the great festival held every twelve years numbers over fifteen million – more than the entire population of one of the world's great cities. Even the influxes of tourists – themselves a kind of secular pilgrim – cannot match these numbers. The physical act of pilgrimage is almost universal: the only major culture from which it is largely absent is Protestant Christianity.

Anthropologists have suggested that pilgrimage is a modern replacement for the ancient rites of tribal initiation, where the individual is first separated from the tribe, then placed in a kind of marginal state, either by living away from the tribe or under a totally different set or rules, and finally reintegrated into society in his new status. Pilgrimage has some of these attributes, but it is ultimately of less concern to society than to the individual. Even on the mass pilgrimages to Mecca or to Kumbh Mela, there is nothing that says that this is a ritual that takes place as a kind of social transition: each of the individuals who make up the crowd is in search of something that, by and large, concerns him alone, and these are spiritual rather than social goals. On his return, he may enjoy increased prestige in his social group – this was once particularly true of the returning pilgrim from Mecca, or *hajji* – but in general terms any transformation which may occur as a result of pilgrimage is not reflected in social terms. In religious terms, however, it is indeed such an experience, stepping beyond the boundaries of everyday life: as one writer puts it: 'If mysticism is an interior pilgrimage, pilgrimage is exteriorised mysticism'. The images of mysticism and pilgrimage are often the same; in particular, the idea of life as a pilgrimage, either in metaphorical or in real terms, is to be found in both eastern and western thought. The most extreme form is related in the *immrama* of the Celtic monks, for whom pilgrimage was a journey without a specific goal, albeit in search of a promised land in the far west; but they followed no set path, travelling where God's will took them. Indeed, setting out into the Atlantic in their frail craft, they could do little else.

In a sense, pilgrimage begins at the moment when men declare one place to be particularly holy; even a short journey to a shrine can be a pilgrimage. When the records of organised religion first appear, the shrines have already acquired a definite hierarchy. Stonehenge is clearly a more important site than any of the long-vanished local places of worship at a sacred spring or tree, and we can hazard a reasonably confident guess than men and women travelled some distance to worship at spectacular monuments like the great prehistoric stone circles. In China, there is evidence of such sacred journeys for the purpose of sacrifice from a very early date, and in ancient Egypt there is some evidence of a kind of occasional pilgrimage, practised by great officials who inscribed their names at the temples they passed. But pilgrimage in its true form, a journey for purely religious reasons, beyond the call of everyday worship, only emerges gradually, perhaps in the fifth century BC in India, and about the same time in the Near East and Greece. The journey to the temple at Delphi in search of the oracle pronounced by the priestess of Apollo is a pilgrimage of a recognisable type: the long journey undertaken in order to solve a material problem. At the same time, we begin to hear of temples sacred to Asklepios, god of healing, which offer a physical cure to the worshipper coming from afar . These are journeys designed to resolve problems of a physical or practical nature; there is a clearly-defined structure of ritual and reward.

It is only with the emergence of the religions which lay emphasis on the spiritual side of man's nature that pilgrimage becomes a devotional or even ascetic practice. There are of course no clear-cut divisions: the pilgrimage can be a devotional one undertaken to fulfil a vow, which in turn originated in a practical problem. A medieval traveller in the Christian west might, on a ship at the height of a storm, vow to go on pilgrimage to a place whose patron saint was particularly favourable to seafarers in distress, such as St Nicholas at Bari. Penitential pilgrimages, too, were a kind of response to practical problems, and indeed in the Low Countries in the fifteenth century, they were a recognised judicial punishment, a kind of formal banishment; but the effect was somewhat lessened by the scale of charges by which a sentence to go to Rome or Jerusalem or some local shrine could be bought off, the price depending on the distance involved. Equating pilgrimage with the payment of a sum of money is the extreme of institutionalised pilgrimage; but in general pilgrimage, by its very nature, defies organisation and institutionalism. There may be certain general rites to be observed, and there may be particular sacred times; but the decision as to when and where to set out remains voluntary and individual.

As a result pilgrimage has always been to some extent free of the control of religious hierarchies, and has often had a popular and even subversive nature. This is particularly noticeable in the rise and decline of pilgrimage centres outside those with special associations, the 'prototypical' sites linked to the founders of religions. From medieval England alone we can cite the examples of Becket at Canterbury, an arch-opponent of the king; of Simon de Montfort, who was the focus of a spontaneous cult after his death, leading the rebel army against the king, at the battle of Evesham; of Edward II, overthrown in a coup d'état. All these were political pilgrimages, focal points for popular discontent. Only Canterbury developed into an orthodox pilgrimage as the political background was forgotten. Popular devotion could create a miracle-working shrine in the teeth of offical opposition, as with the relics of the holy blood at Wilsnack in Germany, which, as we shall see, flourished despite the disapproval of the bishop and the pope. The same spontaneous popular devotion is responsible for new pilgrimage goals in India, for the shrines of local Moslem holy men, but perhaps most dramatically for the famous modern pilgrimages of western Europe, Lourdes, Fatima and Knock, where ordinary believers have asserted, in the face of atheism and materialism, that miracles do happen, and have created new places of worship dedicated to the Virgin Mary at which pilgrims come particularly to seek for cures.

By contrast with these recently sanctified sites, there is another group of pilgrimage places best classed as 'numinous', having an ancient aura of divinity which has persisted through one or several changes of religion. The 'prototypical' sites – Jerusalem, Mecca, Rome, Bodh Gaya – have this quality, but it is overlaid with specific pilgrimage myths, whereas a place like Glastonbury or Lough Dergh or the sacred mountains of China have no such specific 'personality cult' attached, but have nonetheless retained an identity as an especially sacred spot despite the lack of a specific focus. Such places usually have a distinctive physical feature, and here we come face to face with a much more primeval level of religion, the awe inspired by mountains or the sacred nature of water as a necessity of life. Glastonbury, with its prehistoric origins as a cultural and economic centre, appears as a place of pilgrimage in the early middle ages, and after the eclipse of the Reformation, has re-emerged as a focus not only for Christian pilgrimage but also for the followers of the esoteric, well outside the normal boundaries of organised religion, who are also pilgrims to a place which they see as set apart by whatever spiritual system they believe in.

Let us then begin our journey, a pilgrimage though pilgrimages, working from west to east. Although each chapter deals with a major religion, the boundaries are not so fixed as this scheme implies: Jerusalem is sacred to three faiths, Gaya shared by two, and at a shrine in the Indian countryside you will find Moslem, Buddhist, Hindu and Christian honouring the same holy man. So the last stage of our path leads us to look at the pilgrims themselves, without regard for sect or creed; and we shall find a surprising harmony of custom and practice, a harmony which makes pilgrimage a truly ecumenical occupation. The need to set out in physical search of a spiritual goal is one common to all mankind.

CHAPTER ONE

Jerusalem: pilgrimage as devotion

We all think of the world as centred on our own town, our own country, and it takes a great leap of the imagination to see its centre as being somewhere else. Yet for three of the great religions of the world, one city has been the centre of both the spiritual and physical worlds: Jerusalem. If you look at a map drawn by a medieval Christian monk, Jerusalem stands at the centre of the circle: the earth is bounded by the Stream of Ocean, which rings it round, and great rivers divide it into four. Even after this neat diagram gave way to a semblance of realism, Jerusalem stayed at the centre of maps for many centuries. What was the magic of this city, the spiritual magnet for Jew, Christians and Moslems alike, with an identity so powerful that it became the ideal city of life after death, the goal not only of the journey through space of the pilgrim in the physical world, but also of his journey through time in the world of the spirit?

Jewish pilgrimage

Jerusalem began life as a fortress, a stronghold on a plateau high in the hills of Canaan. Its warlike origins have never been far away throughout its history: it fell to the besieging Jewish army under King David to become the focal point of Israel, the promised land; it was rased by the Romans, taken (and its inhabitants slaughtered) by the Crusaders, fought over by Moslem and Christian for a century and a half, and lastly retaken by Israel in our own time. Unlike other centres of pilgrimage, it is not a place of peace, set apart from the world: it has often been at the centre of the political stage, from the moment when David chose it as the symbolic heart of his kingdom, a kingdom fired by a nationalist religion which has no parallel among the world's faiths. The Temple which David raised to house the Ark of the Covenant, the ancient shrine carried with the twelve tribes during their search for the promised land, was a symbol of nationhood as well as worship: and Judaism is unique in its acute sense of place and of belonging, that unity of spirit in adversity inspired by a vision of a physical home, which is at once the wonder and despair of lesser mortals. The absence of an idol intensified the sense of Jehovah's real presence, and all believers went regularly to pay homage to him, in accordance with the command of Moses in the Book of Exodus: 'Three times a year all thy males shall appear before the Lord God.' It was both an ancient ceremony, a journey to the local temple, and a new concept, that there could be a holy place without a physical presence in the form of a statue. Moreover, at a very early date, sacrifices to Jehovah were only performed at the Temple in Jerusalem, and the other temple sites, which had once been almost as important, were denounced by the prophets as impostors. God, for the early Jewish believers, dwelt at Jerusalem, and the journey there became a duty. Four festivals in particular were the occasion for such pilgrimages: Passover, the Feast of Tabernacles, the Feast of Weeks and Chanukka. Of these, Passover was the chief: thirty days before the Passover, the roads were repaired, fountains were uncovered, the sepulchres whitened, bridges made good, and the streets and squares of Jerusalem were prepared for the encampments of the visiting pilgrims. Pilgrims arrived in organised groups, bringing the taxes due to the Temple and the cattle for their sacrifice with them. In the Mishnah, the written version of the traditional oral law produced in the centuries following the destruction of the Temple by the Romans, an idealised picture of such a pilgrimage is given:

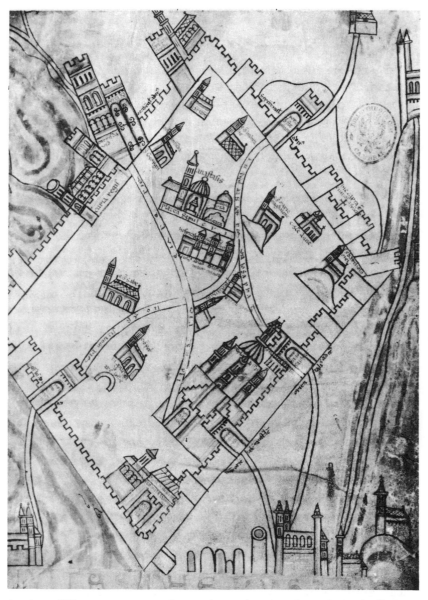

1. A twelfth century map of Jerusalem, showing the principal pilgrim sites. The Temple is at the lower right, the Holy Sepulchre in the upper centre.

In the early morning, the official in charge says: 'Arise! We will go up to Zion, to the house of our God!' From the neighbourhood they bring figs and grapes, dried figs and raisins from further afield. The cattle go before them, their horns adorned with gold, and wreathes of olive on their heads. Flutes play before them, until they come near to Jerusalem. When they draw close to Jerusalem, they send messengers ahead, and set their firstfruits in garlands. The dignitaries and treasurers come out of the city to meet them, according to the rank of the new arrivals...

With the coming of the Roman empire, travel became easier, and pilgrims from outside Israel itself were more numerous. Visitors from the Jewish communities in Egypt and Babylon were unknown before the Roman period, but quickly became commonplace. By the first century of the Christian era, we find a system of guest-houses for foreign pilgrims, linked to the synagogues of the different nations, with rooms and water provided. The organisation of the groups was such that the Temple authorities evidently had some idea when to expect them. In some years, an extra month was declared in the calendar so that Jews from outside Israel could reach Jerusalem in time for the Passover, which implies that the priests there knew more or less when to expect them, and also what progress they were making on their journey. The pilgrims from within Israel had only relatively short distances to travel, days or weeks rather than months, and could thus set out at short notice. They followed traditional routes, provided with watering-places for men and animals. They spent at least one night within the city, and a week or so in the neighbourhood: at Passover there was certainly not enough room for all the pilgrims within the confines of its walls. Feeding the multitudes was not a problem, because they brought offerings with them, but water was more difficult to provide, particularly because part of the ceremonial involved ritual bathing in order to maintain religious purity.

Great festivals were a time for thanksgiving, for example for the birth of a child, and for the ritual sacrifice of a whole beast; and the throngs in Jerusalem were such that during the Roman occupation the garrison was always strengthened during festivals and the governor himself was present. Even if the majority of Jews were unable or unwilling to obey the Biblical command to the letter, it has been estimated that as many as 125,000 pilgrims gathered for the Passover, about twice the normal population of the city in the first century BC. Philo of Alexandria, a devout Jewish writer of this period, saw the pilgrimage both as a test of faith and as an escape from everyday life, themes to which we shall often return:

> And we have the surest proof of this in what actually happens. Countless multitudes from countless cities come, some over land, others over sea, from east and west and north and south at every feast. They take the temple for their port as a general haven and safe refuge from the bustle and great turmoil of life, and there they seek to find calm weather, and, released from the cares whose yoke has been heavy upon them from their earliest years, to enjoy a brief breathing-space in scenes of genial cheerfulness. Thus filled with comfortable hopes they devote their leisure, as is their bounden duty, to holiness and the honouring of God. Friendships are formed between those who hitherto knew not each other, and the sacrifices and libations are the occasion of reciprocity of feeling and constitute the surest pledge that all are of one mind.

But what Philo does not emphasise is the emotional force of such a gathering for the far-flung members of an intensely cohesive and nationalist religion: the reunion of God's chosen people despite their tribulations made the pilgrimage especially poignant.

If the Passover was the most solemn occasion of the Jewish year, the Feast of Tabernacles in the autumn was the most cheerful, and almost equally popular: Flavius Josephus, the chronicler of the Jewish wars against Rome, calls it 'the greatest and holiest feast of the Jews.' Like the Passover, it was another reminder of the journey from Egypt, as the pilgrims lived for seven days in huts made of leafy branches. It was a true festival, with singing, dancing and music beneath huge lamps in the Temple itself; celebrations went on night and day for a week, interspersed with the prescribed rituals. The Feast of Weeks was the occasion for bringing the offerings of first fruits, while Chanukka celebrated the dedication of the Temple.

The intense feeling of the Jews for Jerusalem was shown on other occasions: the bringing of tribute to the Temple, or visits to the ancestral graves. In the first century BC the Day of Atonement begins to appear among the major festivals. Its penitent and mourning atmosphere was intensified after the revolt in 70 AD, when Titus besieged Jerusalem in order to suppress the nationalist uprising of the Jews. He took the city by storm, but gave orders that the Temple should be spared in the final assault. However, a lighted torch was hurled into the sanctuary itself in the last moments of the fighting, and although Titus himself rescued some of the sacred vessels, the Temple was destroyed, and the daily sacrifice ceased for ever. Sixty years later, when Hadrian proposed to build a temple to Jupiter in the city, and, about the same time, forbad ritual circumcision, the Jews made another bid for freedom: this time, the bitter struggle ended with the ploughing of the site of the Temple. Access was forbidden to all Jews, who could only approach as far as the Wailing Wall until the recapture of the eastern half of the city in 1967.

Until AD 70, the Jewish pilgrimage had been both a religious and national institution, a gathering around a familiar centre rather than a departure into the unknown. In this sense it was unlike any of the pilgrimages which we shall encounter in the following pages; but after 133 AD, the second destruction of the Temple, it became a pilgrimage of a familiar kind, a journey to distant holy places. Moreover, from this time onwards the Jewish pilgrims to the Holy City found their way beset with dangers:

the historian Eusebius wrote that 'there were no longer any Jews left within the walls of Jerusalem; every one of the former inhabitants has departed, and the only people in the city were foreigners...' Jews were only admitted to the city on one day a year, and even this privilege was sometimes denied them. However, the strictness of the Roman rulers gradually relaxed as the threat of a nationalist resurgence faded, and by the fifth century AD we hear once more of a substantial number of pilgrims, sometimes enjoying the imperial favour as under the empress Eudoxia from 443 onwards. The Moslem rulers of Jerusalem opened the city to Jewish settlers in 638, and a small community established itself in the southern quarter. By the ninth century, one traditional form of pilgrimage involved the wearing of mourning throughout the journey, to commemorate the destruction of the Temple. We have accounts of three travellers who visited Jerusalem between the ninth and eleventh century. The eleventh century persecutions of the caliph Hakim and the atrocities of the First Crusade put an end to Jewish pilgrimages for a time, and sharply reduced the numbers of Jews in Palestine.

The twelfth century saw something of a renewal, even though Rabbi Benjamin of Tudela, coming to Jerusalem in 1168, found no more than 'about two hundred Jews dwelling under the tower of David, in one corner of the city'. Samuel bar Simson in 1210 was able to identify a large number of historic sites; he describes how he and his companions 'arrived at Jerusalem, approaching from the west side of the town; when we saw it we rent our garments, as custom commands. Our hearts were moved, and we wept...' He ended his book with an appeal to his fellow-worshippers to visit the Holy Land, and the old Jewish communities began to re-establish themselves there; pilgrims began to become immigrants. The first Hebrew work to describe the geography of the Holy Land appeared in 1322. The expulsion of the Jews from Spain in 1492 led to further immigration, though it was not until the nineteenth century that the idea that the ancient state of Israel might be revived became a serious political possibility. In the last century, Jewish pilgrimage has resumed its ancient role of an affirmation of national identity and as a prescribed religious ritual, just as it had been in Old Testament days, rather than a perilous enterprise undertaken by a handful of enthusiasts. The reunion of Jerusalem in 1967 under Jewish rule at last restored full access to the ancient holy sites for Jewish pilgrims.

Christian pilgrimage to Jerusalem

Just at the time when the Jewish people were driven out of their capital and sacred city, a new religion claimed Jerusalem as its spiritual home. It had been the physical home not only of Christ, but also of most of his earliest followers, and the destruction of the city in AD 70 was as much of a blow to them as to their Jewish relatives. However, the increasing number of Gentiles among the followers of Christ were able to approach the holy city when access was forbidden to the Jews. In the middle of the second century AD, not long after the second siege of Jerusalem, Melito, a Christian bishop from Asia Minor, made his way to the Holy Land, though we cannot be certain that he included Jerusalem in his visit to 'the site of Christ's preaching and deeds'. Other fathers of the Church, such as Clement and Origen from Alexandria, seem to have gone to Palestine to study ancient texts and to research details of the New Testament; and there was a notable library at Jerusalem, founded in 212 by Alexander Flavian, which survived into the fourth century AD. A number of notable scholars came as historical rather than spiritual pilgrims, seeking to shed light on the factual side of the scriptures. Despite the increasing hostility of the Roman authorities towards Christianity in the late third century, pilgrimage had become an accepted tradition. St Jerome wrote that 'it would be a long task to try to enumerate chronologically, from the day of the Ascension of our Lord until our own time, the bishops, martyrs and doctors of the Church who came to Jerusalem, believing themselves to be deficient in religion and knowledge and to possess only an imperfect standard of virtue until they had worshipped Christ on the very spot whence the Gospel first shone from the Cross.'

Although the sterner moralists such as Gregory of Nyssa and Anthony the hermit warned against the frivolities of pilgrimage, which easily degenerated into the love of travel for its own sake, the Christians journeying to Jerusalem increased steadily in numbers. When, under the emperor Constantine, the state took a less harsh view of Christianity, the numbers began to increase: in 325, Macarius, bishop of Jerusalem, uncovered the Holy Sepulchre, demolishing the pagan temples which stood on the site; in 326 the emperor's mother, Helena, travelled to the Holy City to search for relics of Christ, and was later said to have returned with the fragments of the True Cross. Seven years later, we hear of a traveller from the western edge of the Empire, the anonymous 'Pilgrim of Bordeaux' who carefully noted the routes by which he travelled and the distances. More important, his description of what he saw in the Holy Land confirms that traditions inspired by pilgrims' visits were well established. He saw the site of the house of Caiaphas, and the pillar of Christ's flagellation: Golgotha, the Mount of Olives (with the stone where Judas betrayed Christ), the grave of Lazarus – all these were well-known and easily identified places shown to travellers. In 336, part of the relics of the True Cross were again displayed in Jerusalem, and in the same year the first Christian churches on the reputed sites of the holy places were dedicated, foremost among them being the Church of the Holy Sepulchre. Constantine seems to have been actively encouraging pilgrimage, and to have been using state funds for this purpose.

With the creation of these places of worship, Christian pilgrims thronged to Jerusalem in the mid-fourth century, particularly at the great festivals of the church's year, and at the feast of the Invention (i.e., discovery) of the True Cross on September 14: bishops, monks, simple folk, all made their way there. Aetheria, a pilgrim who was probably from Spain, speaks of seeing fifty bishops there at once. The pilgrims' devotions centred above all on the relics of the Cross, which were exposed for public veneration on Good Friday and in the week following the feast of the Invention in September. Such was the enthusiasm it aroused that a guardian, the 'staurophylax', had to be appointed to protect it from the crowd. As early as the time of Aetheria, a pilgrim was reputed to have sunk his teeth into the relic, and, instead of kissing it, to have bitten off a splinter.

The more mystically inclined pilgrims meditated at each of the different sites in Jerusalem associated with Christ, and spoke later of visions and revelations: at the simplest level, a vision of a shining cross was seen in 357 above the Mount of Olives and Golgotha, while Aetheria says that every time she visits the Holy Sepulchre 'we see in spirit the Redeemer lying there in a linen cloth, and as we linger there, we see the angel at his feet and the folded cloth at his head.'

At the apogee of the pilgrimage to Jerusalem in the fifth century, there was a whole group of buildings in the city which commemorated the stories of the Gospels, dominated by Constantius' basilica, which opened on to Golgotha, enclosed by a courtyard. The rock of the Ascension was enclosed by a silver rail. To the west, the church of the Holy Sepulchre now contained the chalice of the Last Supper and other relics of the crucifixion. A century later, the church on Mount Sion had the crown of thorns and the lance with which the centurion pierced Christ's side, as well as the stone with which Stephen, the first Christian martyr, was killed. We owe all this information to a pilgrim from Piacenza in Italy, the first of many pilgrims to find a treasure-house of relics at their journey's end, whose glittering contents quite overawed them.

By this time, in the sixth century, the pilgrims' interest was sustained not only by relics of Christ, but also of his mother; Bethlehem, which had also been given a basilica in Constantine's day, and Nazareth were included in their journeys. As the crowds increased, so the stories multiplied: it is interesting to note that most of these traditions of places and peoples stem from the gospels, and not from the 'apocrypha', which were only declared to be of lesser authority than the gospels in the time of Origen, in the early third century. In other words, it seems that many of the traditions appeared in response to the enquiries of pilgrims, rather than through any genuine or lasting local knowledge handed down by generations of Christians. The major sites were readily identifiable and undisputed; but the avid curiosity of the visitors was fed by the lively imagination of their hosts.

Christian pilgrims did not restrict their journey to Palestine to a visit to Jerusalem: they saw their journey as being to the Holy Land, the scene not only of Christ's death, but also of His life, just as Jewish visitors were anxious to visit the sites of Biblical history. The principal goal of Christian pilgrims outside Jerusalem was of course Bethlehem. The stable of the Gospel stories was identified as a cave near the town, perhaps as early as the decade of his death; and by AD 135 it was a recognised place of pilgrimage. When St Jerome knew it in the fourth century, it had been embellished with a great church built on Constantine's order. The crib was the special focus of veneration: so encrusted with jewels was it that Jerome had difficulty in reconciling it with the image of Christ's poverty. Even so, 'with the eyes of faith' a pilgrim like Jerome's protegée Paula might still see 'the babe wrapped in swaddling clothes, our Lord crying in the crib, the wise men at prayer, the star gleaming above, the virginal mother, the shepherds coming at night.' In the seventh century, bishop Arculf describes the cave as being lined with marble; he also saw the rock pool containing

17

the water in which Our Lord was washed after his birth, and the tombs of the three shepherds. By this time, the grave containing the bodies of children slaughtered by Herod (the Holy Innocents) could alse be seen here, as well as the grave of King David.

Nazareth, as the scene of Christ's childhood, was almost equally important to the pilgrim, even though the stories attached to the town belonged more to legend than to the gospels themselves; at the time of Arculf's visit, there were two churches, one marking the spot where Christ's home had stood, and the other the house where the Archangel Gabriel visited Mary. But these were only two among the host of lesser sites which drew the pilgrim to Palestine, and the greatest devotion was reserved for Jerusalem itself. In the end, however eager the ordinary pilgrim might be for the colourful tales and myriad legends that had grown up about the beauty of the women of Nazareth – granted to them by the Virgin herself – or about the ABC in the synagogue there used by Christ himself, it was to the scenes of the climax of the Gospel story that the devout and curious alike returned; there could be no challenge to the supremacy of Jerusalem.

In 543, when a great new church at Jerusalem was dedicated to the Virgin Mary, pilgrims from all over Christendom were present, from France, Britain, Asia Minor, Rome; the city was wealthier and more prosperous than it had ever been, thanks to the veneration and awe in which Christians held it. However, its safety depended not on the numbers of visitors, but on the power of Byzantium. In the first decade of the seventh century the Persian king Chosroes II inflicted a series of defeats on the Greeks in Asia Minor, and in 613 the Persians attacked Syria; in 614 they laid siege to Jerusalem, and after a brief siege stormed and pillaged the city, destroying most of the churches and carrying off the True Cross. Although the emperor Heraclius regained the relic under the terms of the peace treaty in 629, and brought it back to Jerusalem the following year, the Persian siege marked the end of the great Christian era at Jerusalem.

Within three years, the True Cross was back at Byzantium for safe-keeping, in the face of the threat of Arab armies marching under the banner of a new religion, Islam, a religion which was in turn to claim Jerusalem as its holy city. Jerusalem was peacefully surrendered to the caliph Omar in 638, and its new ruler offered tolerance to both Jews and Christians.

Islam and Jerusalem

Mohammed regarded Jerusalem as a holy place, because he saw his religion as the true descendant of that of the Jewish Old Testament, which had been wrongly interpreted by the Jews. God's revelations to Abraham and Joseph were at the root of Moslem beliefs, and Islam was seen as a return to the purity of the ancient Jewish religion. In the first years of Mohammed's mission, he and his followers prayed towards Jerusalem, and only after a later revelation (and a complete break with Judaism) was the direction changed to Mecca. He also accepted the New Testament as a divine revelation, but, just as in his view the Jews misrepresented the Old Testament, so he held that the Christians misread the New Testament: Jesus was a prophet, the last but one in the line, but not the Messiah. Both Judaism and Christianity represented partial truths; only Islam possessed the whole truth.

According to the Koran, Mohammed ascended into heaven, guided by an archangel, and was granted his final revelation by contemplating the face of God. This event was placed from a very early date in the enclosure of the Temple at Jerusalem; he was said to have been carried there by his horse al-Buraq or Lightning, and to have climbed up to heaven by a ladder from the sacred rock. It was as if Jerusalem was the only place where a true prophet could receive such a vision. So the abstract imagery of the Koran was translated into a literal reality, and the first action of Omar when he conquered the city was to search for the site of the Temple; it was found only with difficulty, as the Christians were anxious to conceal it from him, and it was in any case buried under rubbish. A simple mosque was built, which a contemporary Christian pilgrim described as 'a square house of prayer, roughly built of vertical boards and of large beams erected above the ruins.' Jerusalem had begun its next metamorphosis, into 'Al-Quds', 'the Holiness', of Islam, one of the three great pilgrimage cities of the new religion.

Moslem pilgrims usually ranked Jerusalem behind Mecca and Medina, but some writers put them on an equal footing. 'He who makes a pilgrimage to Jerusalem on horseback, will enter Paradise well conducted, and will visit all the prophets in Paradise, and will be envied by them for his closeness to God... He who puts on pilgrim garb for a pious voyage to Jerusalem at the time of Ramadan [the Moslem fast] will gain as much as if he had shared ten campaigns with the apostle of Allah.' To die in the Holy City was a particular privilege: just as Hindus wished to die at Benares or Anglo-Saxon kings at Rome, so for Moslems 'he who dies in Jerusalem is as if he had died in Heaven; he who dies nearby is as if he had died in the City itself.'

The Dome of the Rock was built at the end of the seventh century in a much more grandiose style than Omar's original mosque, following the style of contemporary Greek architecture; it is still the most elegant of all the religious monuments in the city, and despite later repairs and alteration, much of the original building can still be seen. It was the centre of many legends in addition to the story of Mohammed's ascent to heaven, but the mosque built by Omar, 'Al-Aqsa', sited on the forecourt of the Jewish Temple, remained the holiest site of all. It too was rebuilt in stone in the late seventh century, but was subsequently remodelled a number of times, and little of the original survives. Stories were told of its great age: it was said to have been built by Abraham, and with the other buildings on the Haram or Temple enclosure, it became the focus of a series of pilgrim tales as elaborate as those told to Christian visitors. Some of these drew on the Moslem view of the Old Testament: the magical chain of judgement which Solomon hung between heaven and earth in such a way that if you had right on your side you could reach up to it but if you were in the wrong it eluded your grasp, the site of Elijah's prayers, or the scene of Solomon's struggle with the Devil. Others, such as the *mihrab* of Mary at the mosque of Al-Aqsa, presented the Moslem view of the New Testament: it was here that the Annunciation was said to have taken place, and Jesus was believed to have been born nearby, at the site called the cradle of Jesus.

Moslem descriptions of pilgrimages to Palestine are almost as frequent as those of Christians: a typical example is Abu Mu'in Nasir, who set out from eastern Persia in the year 438 by Moslem reckoning (1045 AD). Jerusalem was his first stop on a journey that took him eventually to Medina and Mecca. He reached Jerusalem two years later, during Ramadan, and noted that

> ...the men of Syria...if they are unable to make the pilgrimage to Mecca, will go up at the appointed season to Jerusalem, and there perform their rites, and upon the feast day slay the sacrifice, as it is customary to do at Mecca on the same day. There are years when as many as twenty thousand people will be present at Jerusalem during the first days of the pilgrimage month...

> From all the countries of the Greeks, too, and from other lands, the Christians and the Jews come up to Jerusalem in great numbers in order to make their visitation of the Church of the Resurrection and the Synagogue that is there.

Nasir describes in considerable detail the whole of the Haram area, and recounts the stories attached to each spot. He admires the splendour of the various buildings, and notes that 'the doctors of religion concur in saying that a single prayer offered up here, in this Holy City, has vouchsafed to it the effect of five-and-twenty thousand prayers said elsewhere' – half the rate for Medina, and a quarter of that for Mecca. Only once does he allow himself a personal note: having set out on his journey as a token of his repentance of his former sinful ways, he was particularly moved by the Gate of Repentance 'where David – peace be upon him! – had, through divine revelation, the joyful news that God – glory and praise be to him! – accepted of his repentance; and thereupon David halted at this spot and worshipped. And I, Nasir, also stationed myself to pray here, and besought of God – be He praised and glorified! – to give me grace to serve him and repent of my sins.'

At first the Moslem rulers of Palestine allowed both Jews and Christians to travel freely throughout Palestine. Arculf, a Frankish bishop, visited the Holy Land in the late seventh century, and in the mid-eleventh century, as Nasir noted, there was relatively easy access to the holy sites. But this freedom was liable to be withdrawn on a whim, and in times of weak government the journey could become dangerous. Under Charlemagne we hear of relatively well-organised facilities for pilgrims. Charlemagne had made diplomatic contact with the caliph, Haroun el Raschid, and was able to arrange for hostels to be built in Palestine for the use of pilgrims; and the old roads were briefly reopened. But in 870 a Christian pilgrim from Brittany found that he had to get permission from the Moslem rulers of southern Italy even to set out on his journey; he was not allowed to land at Alexandria, and when he reached Palestine the hostels were only just functioning. A century of darkness ensued, with Arab raiders in control of the seas and anarchy in western Christendom following the break-up of Charlemagne's empire.

Only after 950 do we begin to hear of Christian pilgrims venturing to the East again, particularly with the help of the newly established monastic order of Cluny. The monks eagerly encouraged the idea of pilgrimage, and the rapid growth of the order's wealth and influence enabled them to offer practical assistance through the network of monasteries that came to be associated with the order. Whereas in the past the pilgrims had usually been members of the church hierarchy or particularly devout individuals, we now find secular princes undertaking the journey to the east: the sister-in-law of the emperor Otto I went in 970, and we hear of numerous counts and lesser lords who led groups of pilgrims. This secular leadership was increasingly needed, because conditions in the west made travel insecure: although two or three pilgrims might accomplish the journey alone, it was much more common for pilgrims to travel in bands for safety, often with an armed escort. If an important leader, whether from church or state, announced his intention of setting out, he quickly found himself surrounded by fellow-travellers. The abbot of St Vannes in 1026 found he had seven hundred in his entourage by the time he left Germany, and groups of this size were far from unusual: duke Robert of Normandy, a particular patron of the Cluniac monks, led a huge party of pilgrims in 1035. Other princes with Cluniac connections also undertook the pilgrimage: Fulk 'the Black', count of Anjou, whose personal reputation was far from pious, but who was a great patron of Cluny, went no less than three times. The newly-converted men of Norway and Sweden acquired a taste for pilgrimage with their new faith: already great travellers, a visit to Jerusalem satisfied both their love of adventure and their religious aspirations. Indeed, after Olaf Tryggvason, the first king of Norway to adopt Christianity, leapt overboard in a sea-battle in 1000 AD, never to reappear, Norse travellers claimed to have seen him in the Holy City. Many such pilgrims were members of the famous Varangian guard at Byzantium, a regiment recruited exclusively among Norsemen, for whom Jerusalem was one of the regular local sights.

The journey became easier after 975, with the conversion of Geza, duke of Hungary, to Christianity, and the opening of an overland route through Byzantium and Asia Minor. The monks of Cluny built hospices along the pilgrim roads. There might be temporary setbacks, obstinate local officials, suspicious Byzantine civil servants, or even, briefly, a persecution of the Christians in Palestine by the caliph Hakim, which lasted from 1004 to 1014; but by and large the pilgrimage was no more dangerous than any other long journey.

All this was to change when the hold of Byzantium and the caliphs of Egypt on the east was challenged by the Seldjuk Turks, an energetic warrior race not unlike their contemporaries the Normans in the west. After the defeat of the Byzantine army at Manzikert in 1071, Jerusalem was seized by a local Seldjuk commander, recaptured in 1076 by Egyptian forces, and lost again the same year. The land route from Byzantium to Jerusalem was now dangerous in the extreme, with no central authority and a host of petty lords who saw the pilgrims only as a source of taxes. The emperor Alexius, struggling with some success to restore order, sent envoys to Europe in 1095 to seek reinforcements from what was already a regular recruiting-ground for imperial troops. Their appeal, at a Church council in Rome in that year, emphasised the hardships of native Christians and pilgrims alike in Palestine, and inspired the Pope, Urban V, to drastic action. Out of the peaceful pilgrimage to the East came the preaching of holy war – ironically a concept pioneered by the Moslems against whom it was now aimed.

The savagery, treachery, heroism and religious ecstasy that marred and distinguished the Crusades are not part of our present theme, except to note that the first Crusaders did indeed see themselves as pilgrims, and a large number of unarmed pilgrims joined the army on its march, in response to the preaching of Peter the Hermit, an itinerant monk who had once tried and failed to make the journey to Jerusalem. Some of his hearers believed he was leading them to the paradise of a new Jerusalem, rather than the earthly city; the motley rabble of many thousands made its way to Byzantium before the main body of crusaders, despite skirmishes with the Hungarians and the Byzantine troops in the Balkans. The pilgrims seemed to grow increasing more warlike as they journeyed eastward, and in Asia Minor they went on the offensive, attacking Greeks and Turks alike, until a Turkish army slaughtered them at Civetot.

The organised forces raised by Urban V took Jerusalem in 1099, and marred their triumph by wanton bloodshed. The rules had been changed: toleration was no longer the order of the day, and Jews and Moslems were declared the the enemy. Ousama, who knew the crusader kingdom well, went to Jerusalem in the mid twelfth century, and was given a very different reception by the Christians from that which the Moslems had once given to them: instead of toleration, there was hostility:

A proof of the harshness of the Franks (the scourge of Allah upon them!) is to be seen in what happened to me when I visited Jerusalem. I went into the mosque of Al-Aqsa. By the side of this was a little mosque which the Franks had converted into a church. When I went into the mosque Al-Aqsa, which was occupied by the Templars, who were my friends, they assigned me this little mosque in which to say my prayers. One day I went into it and glorified Allah. I was engrossed in my praying when one of the Franks rushed at me, seized me and turned my face to the East, saying, 'That is how to pray!' A party of Templars made for him, seized his person and ejected him. I returned to my prayers. The same man, escaping their attention, made for me again and turned my face round to the East, repeating, 'That is how to pray!' The Templars again made for him and ejected him, then they apologised to me and said to me, 'He is a stranger who has only recently arrived from Frankish lands. He has never seen anyone praying without turning to the East'. I answered, 'I have prayed sufficiently for to-day'. I went out and was astounded to see how put out this demon was, how he trembled and how deeply he had been affected by seeing anyone pray in the direction of the *Kibla.*

It is interesting, however, that the prejudice was to be found among the recent arrivals and not among the Christians native to Palestine; Ousama's account confirms the criticism of Christian pilgrims, who found the lords of the crusader kingdom all too ready to accept the ways of their eastern neighbours. The Frankish nobles who ruled as kings of Jerusalem held the city for a mere nine decades; but they totally altered the Moslem perception of the Christians. Until now, Byzantium had been a political rival, but not a religious enemy; the Christians from the West were both, and had to be driven out. When Saladin entered the city as conqueror in 1187, there was no massacre, and many of the Christians who could not afford to pay a ransom were set free without one. The church of the Holy Sepulchre was only closed to pilgrims for three days, but the Dome of the Rock and the al-Aqsa mosque were both returned to Moslem use at once.

The Christian pilgrimage to Jerusalem slowly re-established itself in the later middle ages, until by the fifteenth century the mass-pilgrimages were more numerous than ever, with a regular service out of Venice to the Holy Land. Whereas the great pilgrim bands of the tenth and eleventh century had been led by magnates, the pilgrimage now became a much more popular movement, because the lords and knights still thought in terms of the elusive crusade which might yet regain Jerusalem. Only with the fall of Byzantium itself in 1453 did the last hopes of Christian rule in the Holy City die away; but the crusading ideal and pilgrimage had long ago severed their brief and unhappy connection. The travellers in the East might complain of the difficulties of dealing with the Moslem authorities, and the hazards of strange customs in a distant land, but they were rarely hindered to any serious extent: even the brigands who preyed on pilgrims realised that it was to their advantage to disguise their robberies as 'taxes'.

In the late nineteenth and early twentieth century, conditions were easy enough for large numbers of Russian Orthodox

2. Pilgrims about to be baptised by Orthodox priests in the river Jordan, having walked from Russia: a photograph taken in 1908. (Ronald Sheridan/ET Archive)

pilgrims to make their way to Jerusalem, travelling by ship from the Black Sea ports. There had been pilgrims from Russia since the early days of the Orthodox Church, and we have a perceptive and modest account of a pilgrimage from Daniel, abbot of a monastery near Kiev, in 1106-8. They had their own particular traditions, such as bathing in the Jordan in their shrouds and burial caps, and carrying home bells dipped in the river water which would act as charms to ward off thunder.

From 1860 onwards, many of the different Christian sects built churches, hospices, schools and monasteries in the city; commercial tours to the city were available in 1874, and in 1892 the city was linked to the coast by a railway. A contemporary estimate puts the annual number of pilgrims in 1911 at about 15,000, and there was no serious difficulty in reaching the city. A description of Passion Week in Jerusalem by the Swedish traveller Frederika Bremer gives a dispassionate assessment of the behaviour of Christian pilgrims:

> With each succeeding day arrived some new procession of pious pilgrims and inquisitive travellers, the people flooding the streets in all colours and costumes, with their camels, horses and asses. Convents and hotels are full to overflowing. Every day has its festivals and processions to the Church of the Sepulchre, but the crushing and the rudeness of the people render it actually dangerous to life to venture thither without the protection of the Kavasses. At the same time the streets and courts on the way to the Church are occupied with Turkish soldiers whose business is to keep the Christians under control and they do it sometimes in the rudest manner, with blows and pushing them out of the way by force. Nevertheless it must be confessed that the Christian pilgrims are themselves rude and brutish, and cannot be managed by any other means. The Jews ...now are preparing themselves for their Passover at the same time with the Easter of the Christians... with the ceremonial prescribed by the Mosaic Law; but this is done in profound quietness within the family. The Mussulmans celebrate also...their Feast of Bairam...they, too,

eat a lamb, according to the ancient usage...But this also takes place in quietness, and the orthodox Christians, as they of the Greek Church designate these, constitute the peculiarly fanatical and dangerous population of Jerusalem at this time.

The British captured Jerusalem in 1917, and it returned to Christian hands for the first time in seven hundred years. This time there were no massacres, and General Allenby entered on foot, as a pilgrim, to take possession of the city. Little changed; the quarrelling priests who had fought over the Church of the Holy Sepulchre were told the arrangement worked out by the Turkish authorities was to remain, and it was even enshrined in a booklet entitled 'The Status Quo': Armenians, Greek Orthodox, Ethiopians, Copts, Syrians, Roman Catholics and Franciscans all had their minute territorial rights to this or that altar, to the cleaning of this or that sacred spot, to processions at certain dates and times, exactly set out.

On a larger scale, the battle for Jerusalem still preoccupies the twentieth century world: reunited under Jewish rule in 1967, Israel's authority is still not recognised by most of her neighbours, and it is the turn of Moslems to find the shrines more difficult of access. In the modern state of Israel, the gatherings at Jerusalem for the great feasts of the Jewish year are an essential part of national life. But although the Christian and Jewish pilgrims come in greater numbers than ever, the shadow of war still hangs over the city that should be, in an ideal world, the symbol of peace and reconciliation, a worthy goal for pilgrims of whatever creed.

CHAPTER TWO

Mecca

Islam is the one religion which actually commands its followers to undertake a pilgrimage. The Koran states that every believer shall travel to Mecca on at least one occasion in their lifetime, in order to worship at the Ka'bah, the first place of worship, built by Abraham and Ishmael, and later devoted to the rites of idols before it was restored and purified by Mohammed. For centuries, this journey was long and hazardous, involving difficult sea voyages and desert crossings, and only a mere handful of the devout ever succeeded in finally accomplishing the *hajj*; a pilgrim who had not only made the journey but had succeeded in returning home to tell the tale was much honoured. Today the *hajj* has just as much prestige as ever as an act of devotion, but the pilgrims each year are approaching the figure of two million, rather than the few thousand who reached Mecca with the caravans of camels in the last century.

The history of Mecca, in Moslem belief, goes back to the days when Abraham and his fellow-tribesmen worshipped natural gods, the sun, moon and stars. Abraham, however, saw that each in turn could suffer eclipse, and feeling that these therefore could not be real gods, turned instead to the worship of one supreme God, and it was in his honour that he built the Ka'bah. Succeeding generations, however, reverted not merely to nature-worship, but degenerated into the worship of idols; they filled the Ka'bah with their images, and offered sacrifices to them in the shrine that Abraham had built expressly to deny such beliefs. It was these idols which Mohammed overthrew when he cleansed the Ka'bah and restored its rites to their original simplicity. Only a black stone remains as evidence of the pagan past, hallowed for one reason only, that Mohammed kissed it when his work was complete. It is to be greeted with reverence because of the Prophet's gesture, and for that reason alone, not because it has any intrinsic virtue or power of its own. Because of its origins in an idolatrous society, Islam is exceptional among the major religions in forbidding images of all kinds; and this puritan approach extends to the commemoration of the sites associated with the Prophet. There is very little interest on the part of pilgrims in visiting the site of the Prophet's birthplace, or in seeking out the places where he lived in the city, even though Mohammed was an inhabitant of Mecca for fifty-three years before his famous flight to Medina. (This is the *hegira* from which the Moslems date their calendar, and which marks the definitive break with the past. The Christian date was 622 AD.) In any other religion, the places associated with him would be shrines of the highest order. Mohammed's insistence on simplicity, still reflected in the attitudes of his followers, was both his strength and his weakness; admired by all for his way of life, he nonetheless made political enemies because of his reforms, and it was for this reason that he had to leave Mecca, on learning of a plot to assassinate him.

It is therefore not on account of the Prophet's own life that Mecca is the holiest place in Islam, but because it was here that the true religion was revealed to him; and the duty of the believer to visit the city is reinforced by the feeling that this place is in some measure the sacred source of his belief.

The origins of the *hajj* can be traced to the centuries before the beginning of Islam, because Mecca stands on the two great routes which connect the Arabian coast with the hinterland; the passes which run through the mountain wall between the sea and the desert plateau converge on the city. It became, in the early centuries of the Christian era, some five hundred years before Mohammed's time, the centre for a great fair and pilgrimage, the pilgrimage providing a kind of sacred truce among the warring tribes of the area during which it was possible to trade in safety. The town and the surrounding area constituted holy territory, where the caravans from Syria or from across the Red Sea, from Ethiopia, could halt and trade in peace.

The advent of Islam brought little change in this commercial activity, but in addition to the traditional merchant caravans pilgrims came in rapidly increasing numbers as Islam extended its boundaries with extraordinary speed. Mohammed himself had led the pilgrimage nine years after the *hegira* (631 AD). Within a century of the Prophet's death, the whole of North Africa and most of Spain to the west, the Near East to the north, and Iran to the east, was under Moslem rule, and although Mecca lost its political independence, it was now a vastly more important religious centre. The twelfth century traveller Ibn Jubair describes the market at Mecca in the week following the pilgrimage as a vast concourse where every kind of precious object – gems, medicines, silks and jewellery – from throughout Islam was to be seen.

The focal point of the Moslem pilgrimage is the Ka'bah, which now stands at the centre of the great mosque at Mecca. Its history is long and complicated. It is in fact a mosque within a mosque, a shrine about 43 feet high and 36 feet by 36 feet in area. As we have seen, it was originally a pagan temple, reputed to have been built by Abraham in honour of Allah and subsequently defiled by the presence of idols; but its legendary history, and that of the black stone it contains, goes back to the Creation. The site of the Ka'bah is said to have been created before the rest of the earth, which was then shaped by Allah in a series of concentric circles around it, and the Ka'bah is therefore the navel of the earth; the same belief is also found in Hebrew myth in relation to Jerusalem. Adam dwelt on the site of the Ka'bah after his expulsion from Paradise, in a tent made of rubies, and the ritual of walking round it seven times was invented by him in imitation of the angels who circle the throne of Allah. Adam's tent disappeared in the Flood, and the sacred stone was concealed in a nearby mountain. Abraham, guided by Allah, was able to rediscover the sacred site of the Ka'bah, and then built the temple there. As he worked on it, he stood on a stone brought by his son Ibrahim, and left his footprints on it. This is the *maqam ibrahim* which is one of the other relics revered by pilgrims in the mosque at Mecca.

The temple built by Abraham was destroyed by fire and flood, and rebuilt in Mohammed's time; traditionally, this rebuilding followed the form of Abraham's temple, but there may well have been alterations which made what had once been a simple sacred enclosure into a fully-developed temple. In AD 684-5 the temple was destroyed again, during a siege of Mecca; this time it was rebuilt even more elaborately, and covering a greater area, but this provoked controversy among the faithful, and when Mecca changed hands again eight years later, the Ka'bah was remodelled in its 'original' form. The larger temple had had two doorways, so that the interior of the Ka'bah could be visited more easily; but with the restoration of the earlier building, visits were once again jealously restricted. The Ka'bah in its present state is substantially a late seventh century building, much restored; among its foundations there remain a few fragments from the building at which Mohammed worshipped.

Among these stones is the famous black stone, embedded in the wall of the Ka'bah about two feet from the ground, bound by a circle of silver which holds the fragments together. Ibn Jubayr, who visited Mecca in 1183, describes it as follows:

> The blessed Black Stone is encased in the corner facing east. The depth to which it penetrates it is not known, but it is said to extend two cubits into the wall. Its breadth is two-thirds of a span, its length one span and a finger joint. It has four pieces, joined together, and it is said that it was the Carmathians – may God curse them – who broke it. Its edges have been braced with a

sheet of silver whose white shines brightly against the black sheen and polished brilliance of the Stone, presenting the observer a striking spectacle which will hold his looks. The Stone, when kissed, has a softness and moistness which so enchants the mouth that he who puts his lips to it would wish them never to be removed.

This black stone, although it is the focus of the rites at Mecca, presents a difficult theological problem for a religion which so fervently condemns idols and idolatry in any form whatsoever. A celebrated *hadith* or proverb tells how Omar, the Prophet's successor, by whose order the Koran was edited, approached the stone and kissed it, saying: 'I know that you are only a stone, which can do neither good nor evil, and if I had not seen the Prophet (may the blessings and prayers of Allah be on him!) kiss you, I would never kiss you'. This attitude, in which the stone is simply regarded with reverence because of its associations, was not accepted by humbler worshippers, and the legends attached to the black stone multiplied and grew increasingly exotic. It was regarded as an angel sent by Allah to record all the deeds and misdeeds of mankind, which it would then repeat to him on the day of judgement. Alternatively it was a stone with eyes and a mouth which Allah had fashioned especially in order to swallow the document recording the covenant between him and Adam, written on a piece of parchment; it was to bear witness at the end of time whether Adam and the sons of Adam had fulfilled their part of the bargain. It became the eye of Allah, or Allah's right hand on earth, a role not so far distant from the days before Islam, when it had been worshipped in its own right.

The interior of the Ka'bah was very simple, and never seems to have played an important part in Moslem worship or the rituals performed by pilgrims. Although access has been by turns freely allowed and severely restricted according to the prevailing attitudes down the centuries, only the most devout or the

3. Pilgrims at Mecca visiting the interior of the Ka'bah
in the fifteenth century, from Nizami's account of his
journey; the manuscript is dated 1442.
(British Library, Oriental MS 25900, f.114v)

inquisitive have been interested in penetrating to the inside. Ibn Jubayr gives a good description of what it was like in his day:

> In the wall facing the entrance...are five marble panels set lengthways as if they were doors. They come down to a distance of five spans from the ground, and each one of them is about a man's stature in height. Three of them are red, and two green, and all have white tessellations so that I have never seen a more beautiful sight... At the place opposite this, falling back from it three cubits, is the praying place of the Prophet – may God bless and preserve him – and men crowd to pray at it and be blessed. Between each pair of panels is a marble slab of pure and unstained whiteness on which Great and Glorious God had fashioned, at its first creation, remarkable designs, inclining to blue, of trees and branches...each slab is the half of the other, and when the cut was made they divided to make these designs.

Apart from the exquisite marble panelling, there was very little else: two small silver doors and gold engraving on the upper half of the wall. It was a prototype for mosques throughout the Moslem world, where the richness of the ornament and the marvellous handling of space and perspective made up for the absence of all figurative work.

In Ibn Jubayr's day, it was possible to reach the interior of the Ka'bah by a wooden staircase on wheels, set up at appointed times for pilgrims; but it was probably because the small size of the Ka'bah made visits by large groups impractical that it came to play a less and less important part in the pilgrimage. Indeed, the saying of the ritual prayers is forbidden inside the Ka'bah, and a visit is thus a purely personal devotion, and one which today is very rarely permitted. This is in sharp contrast to the beginning of this century, when foreigners could obtain admission at any time on payment of a fee. The only major ceremony associated with the interior of the Ka'bah is the ritual washing of the pavement, which takes place three times a year; one of these occasions is during the *hajj*, but it is done when the pilgrims are absent from Mecca. At this time the black cloth covering the exterior, the *kiswah*, is replaced; in the last century, the new *kiswah* was sent to Mecca by the caliph of Egypt with the pilgrim caravan which set out from Cairo.

The Ka'bah stands at the centre of the great mosque, which, because of the rites which the pilgrims have to carry out around the exterior of the Ka'bah, consists of a vast courtyard with buildings around the perimeter. Strictly speaking, it is not actually a mosque; its proper name is *haram es sherif*, the noble sanctuary, and it lacks the normal layout of a mosque, which is designed with the idea of praying towards Mecca in mind. The daily practices of a mosque, readings and services, copying of the Koran and similar activities, take place in the porticos which surround the courtyard. Originally, the space around the Ka'bah was hemmed in on all sides by houses, and the *haram* was a kind of private square entered from doorways leading from the houses of the leaders of the new sect. With the great conquests of Islam in the seventh century, the flow of would-be worshippers increased considerably, and the caliph Omar bought and demolished many of the surrounding buildings, replacing them with a boundary wall marking out the *haram*. A century later, after further enlargements and demolitions, the first version of the galleries which surround it today were built, and the *haram* was extended until the Ka'bah was surrounded by an equal space on all sides. This work, begun by el Mahdi in AD 783-4, was completed by his successor, and gave the courtyard its present appearance, with an area 180 yards by 120 yards, a surprisingly small area given the vast numbers of pilgrims who come to worship here.

Apart from the Ka'bah itself the *haram* contains half a dozen other small structures. The well of Zamzam, which was believed to have appeared miraculously when Hagar and Ishmael were abandoned in the desert by Abraham, was said to have been rediscovered by an ancestor of the Prophet. In the early days of the faith, it seems simply to have been regarded as a source of water for the *haram*; in the eighth century, a new and purer supply was piped in from the hills, which flowed into a basin in the sacred enclosure; but local opposition to this innovation was such that it was taken out fifty years later, and the well of Zamzam was once again recognised as the sacred source, as it had evidently been in heathen times. It was originally open, but was given a roof and colonnade in the early ninth century. A story relates how the well was restored in the early twelfth century.

Traditionally, no private benefaction was allowed within the *haram*, and works could only be undertaken with the caliph's permission; all that was recorded was that the work was done at his command, and no mention was made of the benefactor on the inscription. The devout were nonetheless anxious to undertake such works, even though large bribes were usually also payable to the local emir. In the case of the well of Zamzam, a wealthy foreigner approached the emir, and said that he wished to repair the well; he offered to provide a clerk who would record the entire expenditure, and once it was complete, he would give the same sum to the emir. The emir greedily accepted, but the moment the work was finished, both foreigner and clerk disappeared overnight, leaving the emir to bewail his lack of foresight; the money had all been spent on the restoration, as the foreigner intended.

Although the well of Zamzam has no formal place in the religious rites, it has a powerful hold on popular imagination; the most sought-after souvenir of the *hajj* is a bottle of water from the well, and pilgrims always try to drink its brackish water after completing their rites. Originally the water was drunk with a kind of fermented mead, prepared in a building next to the well, but this custom had vanished by the time of Ibn Jubayr's visit.

Another pavilion houses the *maqam ibrahim*, the stone on which Abraham stood to set the cornerstone of the Ka'bah in position, and which bears his footprints. It was originally a portable relic, kept sometimes in a chest, and removed in times of danger. It was later housed in a portable iron cage, before the present pavilion was built, and even then it was sometimes moved inside the Ka'bah; Ibn Jubayr saw it there, although the pavilion built to house it was already in existence. Today it serves as the marker for the conclusion of the pilgrim's worship, the point where he makes his two final prayers at the end of his ritual devotions.

This then is the setting for the pilgrimage at the heart of the beliefs of Islam. The *hajj* is enshrined in the Koran, and its place in scripture means that it is much more formal, with a host of specific rituals for each stage and place, than any other comparable pilgrimage. There is nothing in the Christian liturgy that remotely corresponds to the series of prescribed actions and prayers which are associated with the journey to Mecca; and among the eastern religions, only Hinduism has complex rituals to be performed by the pilgrim at a shrine, and these are carried out by just a small proportion of devotees.

Although with the speed of modern travel the journey to Mecca and back can be completed in a week or two, rather than the many months that used to be involved, the emphasis of the *hajj* is still on the need for proper spiritual preparation for the journey. Anyone who undertakes it must first enter a state of *ihram*, vowing to abstain from worldly actions and emotions, and donning a specific garb. Pilgrims must be in *ihram* before they pass the boundary stones which mark the edge of the sacred territory at Mecca, but this is simply the culmination of a spiritual preparation which will have begun months beforehand, and which corresponds in a way with the long and arduous physical journey of the pilgrims of earlier generations. For them, the *hajj* might include time spent with the famous teachers of Islam in the cities along their route; they might come by way of Jerusalem or other shrines. The modern pilgrim has to attain the

4. Pilgrims performing the ritual
circumambulation at Mecca, in front
of the Ka'bah.   (ET Archive)

5. The Great Caravan sets out for Mecca: a mid-eighteenth century
engraving. (Hulton Deutsch Picture Library)

same state of mind as these earlier devotees in much more mundane circumstances, and in a much briefer timespan, but the same ceremonies for the departure of the pilgrims on their journey are still observed, and emphasise the nature of the *hajj* as a separation from earthly commitments.

The rites of *ihram,* which nowadays may take place before the pilgrim has boarded his plane – because he will be inside the sacred boundaries when he lands – include the ritual washing and trimming of hair, beard and moustache, and trimming of nails. These operations cannot be repeated until the pilgrimage rites are completed. Male pilgrims put on two white cotton sheets, one for the lower part of the body and one for the upper, and wear seamless sandals. Women wear plain dresses and cover their heads, but are not allowed to veil their faces. All perfumes, jewellery and other personal adornments or signs of wealth are forbidden, and pilgrims must abstain from sexual contact. They must also refrain from 'abuse and acrimonious disputes' and live in harmony and mutual respect. A series of vows and prayers specify the pilgrims' intentions, such as whether they intend to complete the lesser pilgrimage at Mecca as well as the greater pilgrimage or *hajj* proper, which takes place outside the city. Special daily prayers are prescribed, but the most evocative of all is the *talbiyah,* spoken by each pilgrim as he enters the sacred territory, which begins 'Here I am, Lord! What is Thy command?', and which becomes a kind of password between the pilgrims as it is repeated in the following days.

The visit to Mecca is, as we have said, the lesser of the two rituals, and can be accomplished at any time of the year except for the period of the *hajj* itself. But because it almost always precedes the *hajj,* the arrival at Mecca is a moment which has made such a deep and powerful impression on pilgrims throughout the centuries that the name of Mecca has passed beyond the boundaries of Islam into many other languages as a symbol of the ultimate goal. Arriving at Mecca, today the pilgrim encounters a formidable organisation, created to deal with an influx of two million or more travellers in three weeks, perhaps five or ten times the number of a century ago. The traditions, however, are carefully respected in every detail, and the pilgrims are entrusted in groups to a *mutawwif* or pilgrim guide, whose task it is to see that all the rituals are correctly carried out. These are centred on the sacred mosque, which pilgrims usually enter by the Gate of Peace, before they come face to face with the Ka'bah, standing in the centre of its colonnaded inner courtyard, with the black stone and the other sacred sites, the place where Abraham prayed towards the Ka'bah, the graves of Hagar and Ishmael, and the well of Zamzam. The Ka'bah is covered by a huge black cloth, embroidered with bands of gold calligraphy with verses from the Koran; it is more dramatic in its simplicity than most of the more ambitious shrines of other religions which seek to impress pilgrims by their visual riches. The pilgrims circle the Ka'bah seven times, counter-clockwise, making a gesture of touching the black stone as they pass it, and reciting either the special prayers composed for the occasion or prayers of their own devising. It may seem ironic to the non-Moslem that a central ritual of a religion which, more than any other, is vigorously opposed to images, should be focussed on an ancient pagan altar; but it is precisely the abstract nature of the Ka'bah, its veiled form and the emphasis on unity that make it such a powerful emblem. We have already noted the legends attached to the *haram* and the Ka'bah, but these play little part in the pilgrim's attitude. They are curiosities, only marginally relevant to his purpose.

The *hajj* proper involves a journey to the Mount of Mercy at Arafat, a dozen miles east of Mecca, where Mohammed addressed his followers for the last time; the ritual of *wuquf* or standing at Arafat is the essential part of the pilgrimage, and the whole day is devoted to sermons and prayer. The pilgrims must arrive by daybreak, but as soon as the ceremonies are over, they

6. Pilgrims at Mecca: the Ka'bah is to the right of centre, covered by a black cloth. (Hulton Deutsch Picture Library)

depart as quickly as possible, as required by ancient custom, even though the crush of buses means that the journey of a few miles to Muzdalifah, the next stage of the pilgrimage, will take some hours. Here a ritual prayer is performed, and the pilgrims gather small stones for the next day's ceremony, the stoning of the pillars at Mina. At this point, the pace of the pilgrimage relaxes: the pilgrims spend three days at Mina, encamped in a vast city of tents. The customs here are perhaps the least spiritual of the journey and even devout Moslems find them somewhat at odds with the central tenets of Islam. The stoning of the pillars is not supported by any text in the Koran, but stems from a traditional story about Abraham hurling stones at the devil when he tempted him to disobey God's command to sacrifice his son Ishmael. Each pilgrim hurls forty-nine stones at the three pillars set up to represent Satan; but the enthusiasm of many *hajjis* leads them to throw larger stones or even sandals, shouting curses instead of the prescribed praises of Allah. This is followed by the ritual sacrifice of an animal by each pilgrim, an essential feature of the ceremonies. Originally, part of the animal was cooked and eaten at Mina, and the rest was given to the poor; but a ritual which once showed the pilgrims' readiness to help the less fortunate has become an extravagance and a vast problem in terms of the disposal of thousands of wasted carcasses.

The pilgrimage ends with the rite of *tahallul* or deconsecration, when the pilgrims have their hair cut on their return to Mecca, and a further ritual visit to the Ka'bah, which is this time an obligatory part of the *hajj*. Many pilgrims then return to the encampment at Mina for three days, before making a last visit to the Ka'bah; others go on to Medina to visit the Prophet's Mosque. There is a sharp contrast between the visit to Medina and the ceremonies at Mecca, where the sites associated with Mohammed's life there are not regarded as worthy of interest. Although great care is taken to avoid anything resembling idolatry, Medina displays the relics of the Prophet's life in the city much more proudly, and they are the chief attraction for pilgrims. It is in fact a pilgrimage like any other, a *ziyarah* in Islamic terms, like the pilgrimage to Jerusalem, undertaken out of reverence for the Prophet but not because of any inherent scriptural command. The precautions against excessive reverence for the sites of Medina extend to notices which forbid visitors to prostrate themselves before the tombs of the Prophet and his successors, and this rule is enforced by the local police.

The focal point of the pilgrimage to Medina is the Prophet's Mosque, which ranks second among the shrines of Islam, being also the second oldest place of Moslem worship. It was founded by the Prophet himself soon after his arrival in Medina after the *hegira*, or flight from Mecca. The original building, like that at Mecca, was very simple, made of rough stone and clay, with a roof of palm-branches. It was rebuilt during the Prophet's lifetime, and the direction of worship was changed from the north, towards Jerusalem, to the south, towards Mecca, some years after this rebuilding. On Mohammed's death, he was buried in the mosque, as were the first two caliphs, Abu Bakr and Omar. The Prophet's second building was in turn considered too humble for such a sacred spot, and was rebuilt very shortly after the Prophet's death. Fifty years later the caliph of Damascus rebuilt it yet again, in the full splendour to which the Umayyad dynasty to which he belonged had become accustomed, as the triumphant conquerors of the Middle East. Islam was no longer the faith of an obscure Arabian tribe, but a religion whose leaders could negotiate on equal terms with the Greek emperors; and much of the material and many of the artists and masons for the new work were in fact sent by the Byzantine rulers. The new and resplendent building was regarded with suspicion by traditionalists, who were to be heard murmuring, as Sir Richard Burton puts it, that 'their Mosque had been turned into a Kanisah, a Christian idol-house'. Since this rebuilding in the eighth century AD, the mosque has twice been burnt down and rebuilt, and the present structure is the result of work in the fifteenth century after it had been struck by lightning.

The focal points of the pilgrim's visit to Medina are the *minbar* where Mohammed prayed, within the area of the old mosque, which is marked out by a brass railing, and the mausoleum of the Prophet himself, where the pilgrim says prayers for Mohammed, and greets him; no further gestures are allowed. The devout pilgrim will spend a week in Medina in order to perform the 'forty prayers' which should be undertaken, and which involve attendance at the mosque throughout that time.

The *hajj* plays such a central part in Islam that any lesser pilgrimage is overshadowed; but visits to the shrines of local holy men (*ziyarat*) are a common practice. In north Africa particularly, the visit may well have as its purpose a request for a particular benefit; the popular belief is that such places have a good influence, which can be transferred to the pilgrim's affairs if he visits them. The tombs of Sufi saints, the ascetics of the Islamic world, are also regarded with especial reverence. Much more important, however, is the role of pilgrimage in Shi'ite Islam, the school now centred on Iran which believes that the imams, the direct descendants of the Prophet, were their true spiritual leaders. Chief among these is Hussein, the grandson of Mohammed and third of the imams, who met a disastrous end, killed in battle at Karbala in what is now Iraq in 680; his death is commemorated by all Shi'ites on Ashura, the most solemn fast day of their calendar. Shi'ites believe that the tombs of all eleven imams are a kind of extension of Mecca and Medina, and pilgrimage to them is almost as meritorious as the *hajj* itself. The tomb of Ali, the Prophet's son, at Najaf, is the foremost of these sites; other imams are buried at Mashhad, Kazimayn and

Samarra. Mashhad has some of the great monuments of Islamic art, notably the buildings commissioned by Shah Abbas I at the shrine of Imam Ali-ar-Rida.

CHAPTER THREE

Rome and the shrines of Europe: pilgrimage and miracles

Rome's origins as a place of pilgrimage may seem at first very different from those of Jerusalem, but deep in their history, they share a similar past, as the capital city of an intensely nationalist people whose religion was intimately bound up with their state. But whereas Judaism became in defeat an introspective religion, and Jerusalem was the focus for the longings of a dispossessed people, Rome was the centre of a great empire, and secular success drew in all kinds of new beliefs from the peoples who came under Roman rule. The gods of Rome itself were paid no more than lip-service, and in their place flourished exotic cults from the near East, Isis and Osiris from Egypt and the Persian Mithras, while the emperor himself became a god.

Yet despite the diversity of Rome's temples, it was a religious centre. After the initial impetus of the great era of conquest had brought in the alien cults, the emperor Augustus re-established the Roman religion as part of the panoply of the state; and although we might find it rather formal and lacking in spiritual content, the Augustan reformation worked so well that the cult survived for another four centuries. Men remembered Rome not only as the political capital of the empire, but also as the seat of spiritual authority.

When Christianity reached Rome in the first century AD, its followers met with persecution and martyrdom; they worshipped secretly, and were buried secretly, in the catacombs. But despite the problems posed by living so close to the centre of an intermittently hostile government, the bishops of Rome were soon recognised as among the leaders of the church. The first Christians to travel to Rome went on religious business, not as pilgrims to a holy place; and many of those who have made their way to the Eternal City since then have gone for the same reason. In this, Rome is unusual, if not unique; and the borderline between pilgrimage and a journey on spiritual or ecclesiastical business is often difficult to determine. At any rate, we do not hear of pilgrims going to Rome to visit shrines until Constantine brought an end to persecution. 'Christ illuminated the East with His Passion; so that the West would not be less honoured, He illuminated it in His stead with the blood of the Apostles. Where the princes of the heathen are, there too are the princes of the Church'. With these words Maximus of Turin in the fourth century neatly summed up Rome's claim to eminence. Constantine provided the city with its first great Christian buildings, notably a five-apsed basilica on the site of St Peter's tomb. Churches proliferated, and the graves of the apostles and martyrs began to attract crowds of pilgrims; the catacombs were turned into shrines, and suitably adorned, and were visited regularly by the devout: St Jerome, while he was studying in Rome, was in the habit of going there every Sunday.

Rome's appeal to the Christian pilgrim was undoubtedly more worldly than that of Jerusalem or Bethlehem. The ecstasies of contemplating the sites where Jesus had lived and suffered were absent; there was a profusion of holy places, it is true, but impressive as St Peter's was, we do not hear much of the spiritual experiences which it inspired. The city as a whole was undoubtedly seen as a holy place, and could boast more tombs of martyrs than any other city, over a hundred in all; by the eighth century their remains had been translated, for safety's sake, from the catacombs to within the city walls. Rome was impressive as the capital of the western world and seat of the papacy: the pilgrims who have left descriptions of their feelings on first seeing it speak of its aura of past and present greatness – a popular hymn began 'O noble Rome, mistress of the world' – rather than any spiritual quality. The splendour of the rites celebrated in its churches, the feeling of being at the centre of the world, and, from a very early date, a keen interest in the relics of classical Rome – these were the chief inspirations of the traveller. By the twelfth century, the pilgrim's guidebook to Rome, *The Miracles of the City of Rome*, devoted over half its length to a description in detail of the classical city, freely sprinkled with garbled myths associated with the more important sites. The spiritual side of the city seems to have aroused rather less enthusiasm on the author's part, and his readers evidently shared his viewpoint: the book was an enduring success in both its Latin version and in the many translations.

Another aspect of Rome's attraction as a goal for pilgrims was that penitential pilgrims made their way there to seek absolution from the Pope. The most famous of these is the legendary Tannhäuser, the medieval German poet whose sins at the court of Venus were such that the Pope, horrified, denied him absolution until such time as the dry wood of his pilgrim staff should burst into leaf. His was a 'reserved case', so dire that penance and forgiveness lay in the Pope's gift alone. Originally, such cases had been referred to the Pope because they were particularly difficult and local bishops were uncertain how to proceed; but from the ninth century onwards, such pilgrims swelled the ranks of those going to Rome. Likewise, pilgrimage imposed as a punishment for crimes increasingly involved a journey to Rome.

Just as the flow of pilgrims to Jerusalem was cut off by wars, so Rome too was inaccessible at times to both pilgrims and pope alike: indeed, for long periods of the Middle Ages the popes were in exile, or there were rival claimants to the see of St Peter. But these wars and civil disturbances could not be resolved by crusades; it was the popes' ambitions as secular rulers which all too often lay at the heart of the troubles. New attractions were needed to draw pilgrims; and these, in the thirteenth and fourteenth centuries, took the form of indulgences and jubilees.

Indulgences first appeared in Christian practice about the beginning of the twelfth century. The idea that lay behind them was that a specific good deed could be rewarded by the Church, in the person of the Pope, by an equally specific remission of punishment for sin which the sinner might face in the next world: in medieval belief, the unredeemed sinner went to hell, but the redeemed expiated his misdeeds by an appropriate time spent in purgatory, to 'purge' his sins. At first the terms granted were modest, days rather than years, but by the end of the twelfth century, a pilgrim who visited all the forty churches where the Pope said Mass during Lent could gain almost a century of indulgences; Gerald of Wales reckoned in his account of his pilgrimage to Rome that the total was ninety-two years. By the end of the thirteenth century, the process of one shrine outbidding the next had inflated the figure to nearer a thousand years, merely for the act of visiting the churches; each visit counted, however many times it was repeated. By the end of the Middle Ages, indulgences were openly available for sale, and their abuse was one of the main complaints of the Protestant reformers. What had once been a genuine attempt to encourage simple believers had ended as a canker within the Church, nourished by greed and corruption.

A parallel concept was the jubilee year, an idea which seems to have developed almost spontaneously. The origin of the idea was Jewish, but had nothing to do with pilgrimage: it was a periodic amnesty when prisoners were released and penance was performed for misdeeds. The word passed into the language of Christian preachers as a time when salvation was to hand for those who acted for the faith: St Bernard used it in speaking of the Second Crusade of 1146. It was an idea which was not unfamiliar to a medieval Christian, but there is still something of a mystery as to how the belief arose among the pilgrims to Rome in late 1299 that the next year would be a year of 'Jubilee'; no official announcement was made, but figures for the indulgences available for those who were in Rome on the first of January, 1300, were soon being quoted, and a vast throng crowded into St Peter's on that day. The authorities were taken by surprise, and the Pope did not make the idea official until February 22. Further confusion followed, because his statement offered 'plenary indulgence', or full remission of the penalties for sin; the pilgrims thought that they did not even need to repent or confess their sins, and only later in the year was it made clear that proper confession and penitence was essential for the indulgence to take effect.

This spontaneous celebration brought a greater number of pilgrims to Rome than had ever been seen before; no precise figures are known, but they travelled in hundreds rather than tens of thousands; most of them were from Italy itself, going to Rome on the spur of the moment. The outlying lands of Christendom would only have heard of the jubilee year when it was well under way. Although there were claims that the year 1200 had been celebrated in the same style, these were almost certainly untrue. The idea was, however, too good to be allowed to languish for another century, and the next jubilee was declared in 1350. It attracted equally great crowds, even though Rome had just suffered from an earthquake, the Pope himself was in exile at Avignon, and, furthermore, both the English and French kings forbade their subjects to attend. The jubilee interval was changed to thirty-three years, but the next real success was after the popes had returned to Rome, and the days of rival popes during the Great Schism were over. This was in 1450, when the official record reckoned that forty thousand pilgrims a day entered Rome, to visit the shrines which were at last being restored. The interval between jubilees was finally fixed at twenty-five years, and jubilee years are still a major event in Rome, marked by special rituals: the year begins on Christmas Eve, when the Pope goes in procession to St Peter's and enters by a door which is normally walled up. Although indulgences play a lesser part in Roman Catholic theology than in the heyday of the medieval jubilees, the pilgrims flock to Rome for such occasions, and they rank as one of the most important of the pilgrimage journeys of today. Rome still relies on its ancient appeal, as the city of popes and emperors, to draw spiritual travellers; and its historical claims to be the centre of western Christendom have been reinforced by the recent excavations below St Peter's, which have revealed the original shrine from which the power of the Roman popes derives, the tomb of St Peter himself. The strange mixture of past and present, of petty politics, bustling commerce and high spiritual ideals, which has always characterised the city, is still there today. A crowded, traffic-ridden metropolis may be an unlikely goal for the pilgrim; but there is nothing new in the incongruity, and Rome's appeal is undiminished.

The Christian shrines throughout Europe depended, like Rome, on the presence of relics of saints and martyrs to attract worshippers and pilgrims. The cult of saints' relics dates from the earliest days of the church; we hear of the bones of St Polycarp being gathered up after his martyrdom so that they could be set aside in a place where his fellow-worshippers would gather to celebrate the anniversary of his death. This apparently pagan practice of venerating the relics of the dead was attacked by purists. St Jerome set out the classic reasoning for the defence: 'We do not worship their relics any more than we do the sun and moon, the angels, archangels or seraphim. We honour them in honour of Him whose faith they witnessed. We honour the Master through His servants.'
    This idea was gradually elaborated until the martyrs and

saints became intercessors; the common people prayed to them to use their influence with God, just as they might have approached their local lord to intercede on their behalf with the king. They became the spokesmen in heaven of the ordinary men and women, and attracted a devotion just as intense as the pagan gods who had been their distant forerunners. The relics became not merely objects of veneration, but very quickly acquired miraculous powers of their own. At first this was demonstrated by the cures wrought by 'such objects as handkerchiefs and aprons...after touching the martyr's body'; later, the most prized talismans were minute fragments of relics enclosed in a suitable jewelled case and worn as personal charms. Miracles acted as proof of the relic's efficacy, and confirmed that God did indeed act through the remains of his saints. Equally, disbelief or mockery could be punished: Gerald of Wales comments that 'owing to a certain occult power granted to all relics by God, and owing to a special vindictiveness of Welsh saints, those who despise them are usually punished'.

After Rome, the greatest of the Christian shrines was that at Santiago de Compostela in north-west Spain. In sharp contrast to Rome, the centre of an empire and the hub of a vast network of roads stretching out to the ends of Europe, Compostela was an obscure and difficult place to find: in some ways, the very dangers of the road added merit to the endeavour of making a pilgrimage there. It was not an ancient shrine, nor was there any good reason for expecting it to be the burial place of an apostle, no less than St James himself, particularly as his body was already said to be at Toulouse when the miraculous discovery of his grave was announced to the Pope by king Alfonso II of the Asturias in the early ninth century. St James had already been adopted as the patron saint of the small kingdoms in Spain's northern mountains. These kingdoms were all that remained of the splendid Christian civilisation of Visigothic Spain after its devastation by the Moslems, and the discovery of his grave acted as a rallying-point for local patriotism: we hear very early on of the extraordinary devotion of the inhabitants for St James. The discovery followed what had already become a ritual pattern in the creation of a new pilgrimage centre: *inventio*, the discovery of the tomb or relics by a miraculous revelation, was followed in each case by *translatio*, their transfer to a suitably grand new resting-place. In the case of St James, the city around the shrine built at his *translatio* was sacked by the Arabs in 997, but the shrine was left intact, and his fame, already well-established, continued to grow; we hear of pilgrims coming from France, and there may have been visitors from England or Scandinavia in the early eleventh century. Northern Spain, freed from both Moors and Vikings, flourished under the peaceful reigns of Sancho the Great of Navarre and Alfonso VI of Castile and Leon. The rebuilding of all the bridges and the road from the frontier of Castile west to Santiago was the work of Alfonso VI, and his efforts were more than matched by those of Diego Gelmirez, bishop (and later archbishop) of Santiago from 1100 to 1140. As St James had been an apostle, the bishops claimed to be 'bishops of the apostolic see' and to descend in direct spiritual line from St James, just as the popes derived their authority from their apostolic descent from St Peter. Gelmirez was ambitious enough to try to create a shrine which would rival that of Rome, and was fortunate in that the Pope of the time, Calixtus II, was a Spaniard. What other popes would have seen as potential competition, Calixtus viewed with a sympathetic eye. Gelmirez rebuilt the cathedral at Santiago in the latest Romanesque style, drawing on craftsmen who themselves travelled down the pilgrim roads, and using the considerable resources which he could command as effective governor of northern Spain, and ruler of extensive domains belonging to the cathedral. He was the king's councillor-in-chief, and commander of a substantial army as well; his palace survives next to the cathedral at Santiago, and is on a royal scale.

Diego Gelmirez' ambition brought Santiago into the forefront of European places of pilgrimage, at a time when new shrines were springing up all over Christendom, now that Viking and Moorish invasions were no longer a threat. After the disasters of the tenth century, the ravaged churches of Europe were being rebuilt, and new relics and holy treasures were being found everywhere. The expectation of the Second Coming of Christ in the year 1000 had led to a religious revival which found its expression in practical works when the millennium itself was past, the foundation of new monasteries and even new religious orders. Gelmirez' work at Santiago was part of this movement, but the roll-call of distinguished pilgrims who came to this distant shrine indicates that he achieved more than most of his contemporaries. Some of the pilgrims undoubtedly had an eye on Spanish politics; others were chance passers-by, such as the German contingent who made a brief detour on their way to the crusade in 1147; but the majority seem to have found the danger and difficulty of the journey a positive attraction; Spain was still very much a frontier state in Christendom's struggle with the heathen, and was unfamiliar territory. A journey fraught with such problems was clearly more meritorious than the beaten track to Rome. As late as the sixteenth century, Andrew Boorde declared that 'I had rather go five times out of England to Rome, than once from Orleans to Compostela'. We find William X, duke of Aquitaine, famous as one of the first troubadours with a penchant for bawdy songs as well as a cunning and unscrupulous politician, coming here in 1137; he died suddenly in the cathedral itself on Good Friday, leaving his daughter Eleanor as his heir. Seventeen years later, Eleanor's first husband, Louis VII of France came to Compostela. Exiles from the noble families of Europe also appeared: Henry of Blois, bishop of Winchester and brother to king Stephen, came in 1151, making a vast detour on his return journey from Rome, where he had just been restored to his see. Thirty years later Henry the Lion, duke of Saxony and Bavaria, came here shortly after the German emperor had succeeded in banishing him. Visitors were deeply impressed by the splendour of the cathedral, perhaps all the more so because of its setting in a remote and wild place. The role of Compostela as a national shrine is shown by the respect paid to St James by John of Gaunt when he came to claim the throne of Castile in 1386; his wife Constanza was the heir of Pedro the Cruel, and his expedition was an attempt to uphold her title to Castile. He was able to gain the town by diplomacy, and when the surrender was agreed, the army advanced to Santiago. Froissart describes its reception:

> About two leagues from the place, they were met by a long procession of the clergy, bearing relics, crosses and streamers, and crowds of men, women and children, and the principal inhabitants carrying the keys of the town, which they presented on their knees, with much seeming good will, to the duke and duchess (but whether it was feigned or not, I cannot say) and acknowledged them for their king and queen. Then they entered the town of Santiago, and rode directly to the church of St James, where the duke, duchess, their children and attendants, kneeling, offered up their prayers to the holy body of St James, and made rich gifts at the altar. It was told me that the duke, duchess and the ladies, Constance and Philippa, were lodged in the Abbey and there held their Court.

A century later, a Bohemian nobleman, Leo von Rozmital, who was in Spain on a diplomatic mission on behalf of his brother-in-law, the king of Bohemia, came to Compostela to find the church under siege: the local lord, Bernardo Yañez, had quarrelled with the bishop, whom he had taken prisoner, and the bishop's relatives and their supporters had shut themselves up in the church. Yañez attacked the church on the saint's feast-day, and was wounded in the throat by an arrow; one of Rozmital's entourage attended to him, and as a result the entire party found themselves excommunicated and barred from entering the church. However, peace was made, and although they had to undergo a ceremony of absolution, they were able to visit the shrine. Gabriel Tetzel, who travelled with Rozmital, says that the church was 'a large and beautiful church with costly sculptured stone pillars', but, as a result of the siege, 'at that time it was a wilderness. Horses and cows were there. They kept house there and cooked and slept inside'.

But surprisingly, St James himself was hardly in evidence. His tomb was shown to pilgrims, but unlike most other shrines, there were no personal relics, and more seriously, a rival city, Toulouse, claimed to be St James's last resting place. It was above all the idea of St James, the heroic saint who had led Spain's armies in the reconquest of the peninsula from the Moslems, that inspired devotion. He had first appeared at the battle of Clavijo in the ninth century, then two hundred years later at Coimbra, and most notably, at the great victory at Las Navas de Tolosa in 1212, when the Moorish armies were resoundingly defeated by a small force under Alfonso VIII of Leon. If St James could intervene so powerfully in the affairs of a nation, the pilgrims believed that he could equally help them in their personal affairs, whether on a simple practical level or when all other hope had gone, through a miracle.

Christianity, more than any other major religion, enshrines miracles as part of its central belief: just as the miracles in the New Testament are proof of Christ's authority, so the power of the individual saints was judged by the ability of their relics to work miracles. A subtle distinction was made between Christ and the apostles, who could work miracles while they were alive, and the saints, who could generally only do so after their death, when their sanctity was known to be real. Miracles played an important part in the conversion of St Augustine: he witnessed the *translatio* or reburial of the martyrs Protasius and Gervasius in Milan in 386, and the miracles that followed – a blind man restored to sight, a madman cured. Thirty years later, he acquired the relics of St Stephen for his church at Hippo in North Africa, and a series of miracles ensued.

Once such wonders had begun to be recorded, it is not surprising that men and women sought out the shrines where they had happened. There was a further reason why this new form of devotion should flourish: with the triumph of Christianity, the old pagan customs had fallen into disuse, among them the temples of Aesculapius, the god of healing. As so often in the development of religion, the rituals of an earlier faith underlie the emergence of new practices in the belief which succeeded it. The traveller who had once gone to Aesculapius to offer thanks for recovery or to seek a cure now became a pilgrim to a saint's shrine.

This was a very different kind of expedition to the devout remembrance of Christ implied in the journey to the Holy Land; but it was the commonest form of pilgrimage in the Christian world of the Middle Ages. The power of local saints or deities to relieve human suffering and problems recurs in Hindu and Buddhist worship, but the cult of wonder-working relics was a peculiarly Christian phenomenon. The church was innately suspicious of anything that resembled idol-worship, and although a number of wonder-working images and icons did reappear in the later Middle Ages, relics took the place of images of the pagan gods as physical objects on which the pilgrim could concentrate his religious feeling and prayers. Even St Augustine, who had so fervently recorded the miracles at Hippo, began to have his doubts, in the *Retractions* he wrote in his old age. The eighteenth century historian Edward Gibbon, no lover of religion or its ceremonies, paints a lurid but believable picture of what might have happened at a shrine in the fifth century on the saint's feast-day, and imagines the despair of Christians of an earlier age had they been present:

> As soon as the doors of the church were thrown open, they
> must have been offended by the smoke of incense, the perfume

of flowers, and the glare of lamps and tapers, which diffused, at noon-day, a gaudy, superfluous, and in their opinion, sacrilegious light. If they approached the balustrade of the altar, they made their way through the prostrate crowd, consisting, for the most part, of strangers and pilgrims, who resorted to the city on the vigil of the feast... Their devout kisses were imprinted on the walls and pavements of the sacred edifice; and their fervent prayers were directed, whatever might be the language of their church, to the bones, the blood, or the ashes of the saints, which were usually concealed by a linen or silken veil from the eyes of the vulgar.... The walls were hung round with symbols of the favours which they had received: eyes, and hands, and feet, of gold and silver; an edifying picture, which could not long escape the abuse of indiscreet or idolatrous devotion, represented the image, the attributes and the miracles of the tutelar saint.

So, precisely at the point when Christianity was established as the new official religion of the Roman Empire, it took over the local network of shrines of its pagan predecessor; the underlying beliefs had changed very little. The saint's body or relic acquired all the attributes of the old gods: power to heal, power to grant requests, power to transfer its healing attributes to objects which had touched it; but it could also bring retribution to those who offended against it. (At Compostela, anyone who denied that St James's body lay in the altar-tomb there was immediately struck with madness.) In the eleventh century, when travel began to be possible again over long distances without fear of the Viking or Arab marauders who had ruined so many cities and churches, the success of a pilgrimage church depended on the reputation of its saint; the more powerful the saint, the more likely he was to be able to help, and his power could only be judged by his record in performing miracles and in answering prayers. So the keepers of each shrine began to record the miracles and answered prayers, much as Augustine had noted the miracles at Hippo, but with a wider ulterior motive in view. A great monastery would systematically collect relics, so that if a pilgrim failed to obtain a cure from one saint, there were a dozen others on the spot to whom he might turn.

The most remarkable instances of miracles were usually associated with a dramatic event, almost always a real or imagined martyrdom; these served to establish the credentials of the new saint. The murder of Thomas Becket in Canterbury Cathedral on 29 December 1170 sent a shock-wave throughout Christendom: within a decade the new martyr was honoured as far afield as Sicily. At home, however, there were political dimensions to the murder, in which Henry II was implicated, and it is fascinating to see what happened. Becket had been popular in his diocese and was an immediate candidate for sainthood, but the knights who had murdered him were powerful, and the king would not welcome the canonisation of his opponent. So although the first miracle was recorded on the night of the murder, the body was hastily buried and the few relics put in a safe place, while the cathedral had to be closed because of the unthinkable sacrilege which had occurred there. But popular interest was all the greater, and miracles in Becket's name were recorded as far away as Gloucestershire within a month of his death. Many planned to make the pilgrimage, but were unable to do so until a year later, when the church was reopened; six months later, two scribes were needed to record the number of marvels that were happening daily among the throngs of pilgrims at the tomb. These early miracles formed part of the case for Becket's canonisation, which was announced in February 1173. The two major collections of miracles cover the first decade after Becket's death, and contain 703 reports; no other shrine can match this record, even over a much longer period. What is most intriguing is the way in which the pattern of visitors to the shrine changes. Before the cult became official, it was mostly poor folk of humble origin and women who made up the pilgrims; it was thus a genuinely popular movement

7. The Wife of Bath, from a fifteenth century MS of Chaucer's *Canterbury Tales*: a wealthy lady for whom pilgrimage was a diversion as much as a religious activity. (Cambridge University Library, MS Gg.4.27, f.222)

8. John Lydgate, author of the *Life of St Edmund*, prays at St Edmund's shrine: a rare late medieval depiction of a saint's shrine. (British Library, MS Harley 2278, f.9)

which established the shrine's reputation, even if greater men, whose visits would have aroused comment, may have been deterred by the fear of the king's wrath.

What was the nature of the miracles which were reported from the shrines, and what were the pilgrims seeking? The desire to witness or experience a miracle was the principal motive for many pilgrimages. Given the rudimentary nature of medieval medicine, and the difficulty of getting such medical advice that was available, most people relied on a strictly limited range of traditional remedies for their ailments, and the rate of recovery from serious illness was very low. In such circumstances, the Church's positive exhortations to seek out a heavenly doctor rather than an earthly one, which had perhaps originally been meant as a reminder that spiritual health was more important than bodily well-being, came to be regarded as an injunction to leave medical cures in the hands of God and His saints. Indeed, those who attempted a physical cure were sometimes regarded as trespassing on the saints' territory; and conversely even the most mundane recoveries were regarded as the work of higher powers, and might lead the sufferers to make a pilgrimage to record their thanks to 'the holy blissful martyr, that had helped them when they were sick'. The pilgrimage as thanksgiving for assistance, whether miraculous or otherwise, was thus a very common motive, and it is often difficult to draw the borderline between the ordinary intervention of the saints in everyday life in response to prayer, and a miracle. The more enthusiastic recorders of miracles were only too happy to gather in everything that came their way, but more sober writers realised that a surfeit of miracles was self-defeating. So many marvels were reported at St Swithin's shrine at Winchester in the tenth century, when the saint underwent a *translatio* to a new shrine, that the monks themselves confessed they were weary of them. And frequency led inexorably to exaggeration, so that there was a natural reaction of disbelief. Becket's miracle-recorders were careful – in the early years at least – only to record well-attested miracles; lesser episodes might be included among the saint's 'light-hearted acts' or *jocula*, such as the girl from the little Suffolk village of Ramsholt who had forgotten where she had put a cheese. At her small brother's suggestion, she prayed to St Thomas (who had recently cured their priest's daughter of a sore on the face). He duly appeared to both of them in a dream, and reminded them that the cheese was in an old jar. The children and their priest duly went to Canterbury to give thanks, 'where almost everyone to whom he told the story smiled at it'.

Many of the early miracles at Canterbury were cures of local people, well-known to the monks, who needed no testimony as to their earlier ill-health: a beggar who had been blind for two years and who was a familiar character in the streets of the town, or the sons and wives of reputable citizens. These were people turning to their local saint; when pilgrims arrived from distant places, their stories had to be checked more carefully, as in the case of Samson from Oxfordshire, who had lost the power of speech five years previously and could only mouth words incoherently, so that everything had to be repeated several times before he could be understood. After a relatively long stay, he was almost entirely cured, and inquiries were made as to the truth of his story; it was confirmed by a man with whom he had stayed at Rochester.

Samson was one of the many pilgrims who had travelled in the hope of a cure; many others, like the children from Ramsholt, travelled to give thanks, in which case the monks would enquire into their credentials before recording their experiences as the work of the saint. The early stories are carefully documented, just as the inquisitors sent to investigate the case for a saint's canonisation would be rigorous in excluding doubtful ones. But as the pilgrimage grew in popularity, the stories grew less realistic; here, as at any shrine, the folklore of pilgrims took over from conscientious efforts to analyse the saint's posthumous deeds. Among the crowds of visitors, a recovery from a minor ailment made little stir: this was the daily routine of such a place, and there was always a demand for some sensational event. So the stories become more fantastic, and the evidence vaguer, until the shrine itself begins to fall into disrepute and a new centre takes over.

Only a handful of pilgrimage centres succeeded in retaining their popularity throughout the Middle Ages. Even a great shrine like Canterbury suffered a sharp decline after 1420, while small cults might disappear almost entirely. On the other hand, new candidates were always to hand, and from the fourteenth century onwards there was an increasing tendency to concentrate on places which had relics of Christ himself or of the Virgin. The growing enthusiasm for the cult of the Virgin from the eleventh century onwards was reflected in the appearance of wonder-working images. At Notre-Dame de Boulogne, a pilgrimage started almost spontaneously in 1211, and this was typical of many Marian shrines: the installation of a new image was in itself enough to attract pilgrims, and if the statue was said to have spoken or moved, the crowds could be enormous. These were purely popular occasions, a gathering of the faithful from nearby towns and villages, and they often had to be suppressed by the authorities; even if they were tolerated, the cult might well fade in a few years. We find examples of this sudden appearance and disappearance of a pilgrimage centre as far afield as a small village in Lincolnshire in the fourteenth century, and its equivalent in central Germany two hundred years later. The vicar of Kernetby reported in 1316 that 'there have suddenly and unexpectedly arisen new offerings in the said church, in honour of God and the most glorious Virgin Mary, at a certain new image of the said Virgin there'. At Tynbach near Würzburg a pilgrimage began and ended within the space of a few weeks in the late fifteenth century: none of the stories which drew the crowds were recorded, but the church, built with their offerings, remained as evidence.

The great centres of devotion to Mary were on a quite different plane; Chartres, for example, had claimed to possess her tunic since the eleventh century. Yet, unlike other places of pilgrimage, it was statues of the Virgin which drew crowds, just as they had done at a much humbler level at Kernetby and Tynbach. The Virgin of Montserrat, on a spectacular mountain top in Catalonia, the Virgin of Rocamadour, in equally dramatic surroundings in central France, Our Lady of Walsingham in the Norfolk countryside may have originally begun from humble rural devotions, but they achieved a fame out of all proportion to the size of the small country towns which housed them. The 'black' Virgins, believed to be images of great antiquity, enjoyed particular esteem: Montserrat and Rocamadour came into this category, and there was another famous 'black' Virgin at Le Puy in the Massif Central. As with Compostela, difficulty of access added merit to the pilgrimage.

Popular pilgrimages, as we have noted, could be suppressed by the authorities. Sometimes this was for political reasons, as with the attempts to suppress Becket's cult, or, more successfully, the cult which made the rebel Simon de Montfort's tomb a place of pilgrimage. On other occasions, it was because there was a danger of heresy or uncontrolled religious fervour. The church at Wilsnack in eastern Germany was the scene of a highly unofficial cult, which was twice suppressed and frequently condemned from the pulpit, but which survived until the Reformation. The episode which started the pilgrimage occurred in 1383, when a fire destroyed the church and the priest claimed to have found three consecrated hosts in the rubble, intact but with drops of blood on them. The sensational story at once attracted crowds, and a new church was quickly built with their offerings, and with the blessing of the authorities. However, the pilgrimage attracted large numbers of poor people: the crowds became hysterical and uncontrollable, and there were strong suspicions of frauds among the miracles reported. The reformer John Hus reported very unfavourably on the cult while he was still a member of the orthodox church, and it was alleged that a heretical form of worship of Christ's blood was developing, though it seems to have been no more than an over-enthusiastic if rather simple-minded devotion. But the shrine remained open, and it was only some sixty years after the original event that the local archbishop submitted a report to the papal legate Nicolas of Cusa which led to the suppression of the pilgrimage on the grounds of fraud, deliberately encouraged religious hysteria and the display of false indulgences. Yet the popular belief in the miracles at Wilsnack could not be gainsaid: twenty-five years later, in 1475, a great throng of children made a pilgrimage to 'the Holy Blood of Wilsnack', and this event was repeated in 1486, until preachers actually condemned the wickedness of going to Wilsnack from the pulpit. Only the destruction of the miraculous hosts by the Protestants in 1552 put an end to the cult.

Other pilgrimages stemmed from social discontent, and this may have been partly at the root of the events at Wilsnack. The most dramatic of these movements were the popular crusade which preceded the official expedition on the First Crusade, and the famous Children's Crusade of 1212, when two bands of children set out simultaneously in France and Germany for the Holy Land, only to end in the one case in slavery in North Africa and in the other with starvation in northern Italy. Children made a pilgrimage to Mont St Michel in 1333 from May to July, after the phenomenon known as St Elmo's Fire had been seen playing round the spire of the church at Whitsun, and this pattern was repeated at intervals in the next century and a half, culminating in a great concourse of children from Germany and Flanders at Whitsun in 1457. These spontaneous pilgrimages were regarded with deep suspicion by the authorities, who saw them as the

9. The principal shrines of Western Europe.
(Reproduced from Mary Lee Nolan and Sidney Nolan, *Christian
Pilgrimage in Modern Western Europe*, by permission of University
of North Carolina Press)

products of idleness, or, more charitably, as a reluctance to beg from close neighbours; there was always a kind of mass hysteria about them, rather than the deliberate and considered decision which the Church regarded as essential to true pilgrimage.

Other cults could arise from more sinister popular attitudes. The case of St William of Norwich is a striking but by no means unique example. In 1144 a boy named William, an apprentice in Norwich, was found murdered in a wood just outside the town. His family declared that the Jews had seized him, tortured him and murdered him. Ten years later the story had become even more loaded, for the chronicler at Peterborough wrote that 'the Jews of Norwich bought a Christian child before Easter and tortured him with all the torture that Our Lord was tortured with; and on Good Friday hanged him on a cross on account of Our Lord, and then buried him'. But immediately after William's death there was relatively little interest in the case; his story seems to have been deliberately taken up by a new bishop, William Turbe, who was consecrated in 1146 or 1147, and in 1150 one of the monks convinced his fellows at the cathedral priory that the boy's body should be reburied in the chapter house. This was duly done, and a series of miracles followed: William was never officially canonised, but his strange cult, rooted only in the manner of his death and hence in pure anti-Semitism rather than any personal merits he may have had, survived until the Reformation. His tomb attracted little more than local attention, but 115 miracles were recorded there in the period 1150-1170, and for this brief time he was a major figure in the English pilgrim's calendar.

Miracle-working saints and their images were of course one of the principal targets of the Protestants at the Reformation, and many who remained within the Roman Catholic church were uneasy about the spurious claims so often put forward. In England and Germany the relics, fraudulent or otherwise, and the statues were swept away. Some of the statues were found

10. The shrine at Fatima in Portugal during the Holy Year of 1951, when over a million pilgrims visited the shrine. (Hulton Deutsch Picture Library)

to have mechanisms by which they could be made to move, a common enough feature of figures designed to be used in religious processions; but the reformers took this as renewed evidence of trickery, attempts to gull the innocent into seeing a miracle. But even in the most conservative countries, Italy and Spain, there was an eventual reaction; the devotion to particular cults and images no longer attracted long-distance pilgrims as it had once done. The Counter-Reformation curbed the remaining excesses in the sixteenth century, and pilgrimage once more became respectable after the Council of Trent (1545-1563). The tradition flourished, unobtrusively and on a generally local level until the French Revolution and Napoleon's wars. New pilgrimage churches continued to appear, most notably the superb baroque churches of south Germany where there has been a continuous pattern of development of pilgrimage shrines since the Middle Ages. The splendours of the eighteenth-century rebuilding of the late medieval shrine at Altötting, dedicated to the Virgin Mary, bear witness to this continuity, as do the large numbers of completely new shrines founded in the area between 1550 and 1800.

Indeed, there is a remarkable continuity in the pattern of pilgrimage in Europe if we measure it by the rate of foundation of new shrines. More new shrines were established in the seventeenth century than at any other period, and the rate at which new shrines appeared in the periods 1200–1500 and 1700–1900 is not very different. Almost no new Protestant pilgrimage centres have appeared since the Reformation, and all the modern shrines have been founded within a smaller area, yet they are just as numerous. So perhaps it is wrong to see Christian pilgrimage as a primarily medieval institution, but very much as a part of the post-Reformation culture of Roman Catholic Europe.

The motives behind much of modern Christian pilgrimage are best described as an extension of ordinary religious devotion. It may be, at the simplest level, no more than a desire to visit other religious centres, the same kind of curiosity that drives the tourist to seek out monuments of art or history, but with a different and more personal subject as its focus. The pilgrims may be organised in the same way as cultural tourists, and may often combine the two roles. Such pilgrims will usually be attracted by ancient and spectacular places rather than humble local shrines.

More specifically religious motives may nonetheless mix secular pleasures and religious duties, such as pilgrimages to sites with a tradition of local festivities on a saint's day, the Breton *pardons* and the *romérias* of Spain and Portugal being examples. These are holidays in both senses of the word, holy days and a time for pleasure and relaxation. The Portuguese National Tourist Office surveyed the *romérias* of Portugal and classified only one in eight as strictly or essentially religious. By contrast, the German pilgrimages have little or no secular element, the only colourful feature of the Bavarian pilgrimages being the wearing of traditional dress. This, although it seems picturesque to the casual onlooker, simply represents the way in which a conservative society shows its respect for the occasion. Whether secular or strictly devotional, this type of pilgrimage is essentially a communal affair, centred on the local inhabitants and on a local centre of worship.

The individual vow of pilgrimage is probably much rarer – at least in proportion to the total number of pilgrims – than it was in earlier centuries. A typical instance of such a vow would be a response to a prayer answered at a critical moment by the intervention of a saint or of the Virgin; when the pilgrim reaches the shrine, he or she leaves an *ex voto* or votive offering which commemorates his or her deliverance. *Ex votos* may nowadays be photographs rather than the inscribed tablets or models related to the incident – fine ship models were not uncommon – and special rooms are sometimes set aside to store them, often simply because there is no more space near the altars. The great age of votive tablets was from about 1880 until about 1930, and the walls of many chapels are literally covered from floor to ceiling with them. The Roman Catholic custom of burning a candle in honour of Our Lady or of a saint is also associated with pilgrimage, and the candles may be so elaborate that they are preserved rather than used; at some Bavarian shrines, candles dating from the Middle Ages are part of their treasures.

The most striking *ex votos* are those which bear witness to the strongest motive for individual pilgrimage: healing. Despite the advances of modern medicine, the flow of pilgrims to the great healing shrines continues unabated; and the benefits that often result from such a journey, even if there is no miraculous cure, have in turn influenced modern medical thinking, which now tends to take a less mechanical view of illness, and to attribute a clearer role to psychological factors. This is among the oldest and most persistent of all the reasons for pilgrimage: the Greek or Roman pilgrim who sought out a temple dedicated to Aesculapius, would in a number of cases still find a healing shrine on the same site were he able to revisit it today. And, within, he would find similar mementoes, models of limbs or features, to indicate the diseases which had been cured. Such cures are the most frequent form of miracle, from the beginning of Christianity to the present day, and their occurence is almost a prerequisite if a new shrine dedicated to the memory of a reputed but not yet recognised saint is to gain official acceptance.

Modern European pilgrimage is also very heavily biased towards the cult of the Virgin. Of the six thousand or so active shrines, two-thirds are dedicated to Mary; if those where she is a secondary figure are included, four out of every five shrines include some level of devotion to her. It is therefore hardly surprising that almost all of the major centres which have sprung up in the last one hundred and fifty years centre on devotion to the Virgin Mary, and have begun with visions. Lourdes, Knock, Fatima and, most recently, Medjugorje in Yugoslavia all bear witness to the popular devotion to the Virgin; in each case, official reaction was initially sceptical, if not downright hostile, but the Church's caution was understandable, and the acceptance of the new shrines after careful investigation served to enhance their attraction to the ordinary pilgrim. Fatima is perhaps the most mystical (and also the most controversial, because of the cryptic messages said to have been given by the Virgin to one of the group to whom she originally appeared); both it and Knock became focal points for local Roman Catholics when their faith was politically under pressure, and had a distinct nationalist element. The same political element is in evidence at Medjugorje, where the Communist opposition to religious worship made the publicity attached to the apparition of the Virgin in 1981 an act of defiance against the regime. The famous Polish pilgrimage to the Black Virgin of Czestochowa had a similar anti-Communist and nationalist appeal. Now that the threat of persecution is past, their appeal is more broadly based. While Fatima is famous for its annual festival and is often associated with penance, Knock and Lourdes are for prayer and healing. Lourdes has no rival in any religion as a place of healing; from the very first, miraculous cures were recorded there, and it has become the symbol of hope when all earthly help has proved unavailing. Even with the marvels of modern medicine, the idea of pilgrimage as a quest for healing, so deeply embedded in Christian tradition, still has its place.

CHAPTER FOUR

Benares and the shrines of India: pilgrimage as ritual

Pilgrimage plays almost as important a role in Hindu religious practice as it does in Moslem ritual, but it is far more diffuse. Instead of the one great centre, Mecca, there is a vast range of sacred sites: rivers, temples, cities and even the dwellings of holy men. There are perhaps one hundred and fifty major pilgrimage centres in India, and entire rivers are regarded as sacred; the word *tirthayatra* itself meant originally 'journeys to the sacred fords', but is now used generally of pilgrimages. The Ganges is the foremost of the seven sacred rivers; there are seven holy cities, and four 'dhamas' or major dwelling-places of the gods. The dhamas are on the four sides of the Indian sub-continent: Badrinath is in the Himalayas, Ramesvaram in the extreme south, Puri or Jagannath on the east coast and Dvarka on the west coast. From early times, the idea of pilgrimage included that of a tour of the major sites, a circular journey rather than an expedition to one city or shrine. The journey itself is regarded as the experience, rather than arrival at a particular point for a specified purpose. The various staging posts on the journey are divided into *jalatirthas*, the river or water sites where the chief ritual is self-purification by bathing, a ceremony which has few parallels in pilgrimages elsewhere, or *mandiratirthas*, which are usually temple sites where vows and prayers are offered up, much as in other pilgrimage traditions. Even more general are the *ksetras*, holy places or regions: the whole of the Himalayas is a *ksetra*, an area where the activities of the gods may be detected;

the pilgrim, if he approaches the area in the right way, may hope for direct involvement in the divine world.

At a lower level, corresponding to the complex relationships between the great deities and the lesser gods and goddesses who represent 'aspects' of these major powers, are the local temples. Sakti, the mother goddess who appears as Kali, Sarasvati, Durga and others, has special sites of worship called *pithas*, and a Hindu legend relates how these *pithas* came into being. The goddess Sati, married to Shiva, was insulted by her father when he failed to invite either her or her husband to a great sacrifice which he held. Sati went nonetheless; her father abused her, and in despair she took her life. Shiva killed his father-in-law in revenge, and, with Sati's body on his shoulders, began a furious dance which threatened to destroy creation. The gods caused Sati's body to fly apart, and Shiva grew calm; the places where the fragments of her body landed became the sacred *pithas*.

The pilgrimage sites sacred to Shiva have a similar legendary origin: Shiva, in mourning for Sati, is said to have committed some grave sexual offence as a result of which he was castrated, and his phallus was transformed into an object of worship which represented him. Again, there is a series of major and minor shrines associated with the worship of Shiva in the form of a phallus. There are twelve major sites, designated according to tradition by the god himself, and about seventy lesser sites, where the image housed in the temple is said to have come into existence without human intervention. Furthermore, five linked temples in southern India represent the god in the form of the five elements, earth, water, fire, air and ether.

Both Shiva and Sakti present a series of contrasts to the worshipper, since they embody both the benign and terrible aspects of their nature. A pilgrim will seek favours from Sakti, but is equally aware that she can send death as well as life. The majority of pilgrims seek mundane favours – health, fertility, long life – but for the more spiritual devotee worship of both Sakti and Shiva leads to meditation on the nature of life and death, and the attempt to escape from the cycle of death and rebirth by gaining a true insight into reality. In the case of the temples of Vishnu, there is less emphasis on the practical benefits of pilgrimage, because his temples are seen as representing the presence of the divine among men, and are often associated with particular holy individuals. The older temples, such as that at Gaya where the god's footprint is worshipped, are associated with Vishnu's ten *avatars*, the ten forms in which Vishnu appears in order to preserve creation from the threat of destruction by gods or demons. Krishna, the eighth of these avatars, has a particularly strong following, and is regarded in some places, for instance Bengal, as the supreme aspect of Vishnu and the chief among the gods. He in turn is said to have had various incarnations, in the form of sages and holy men. The temples of Vishnu are very much places of meditation and the devotional practice of *bhakti yoga*, which may include joyous celebration as well as quiet thought; they are not concerned with physical well-being, as in the case of the shrines sacred to Sakti, but with spiritual development. This worship of holiness and holy individuals is even extended to saintly individuals of other religions, Buddhist, Moslem and Christian. This is particularly noticeable where a large Moslem minority is present; the tombs of such holy men or *pirs* are the equivalent of the Christian veneration for saints' shrines, but while the Christian sees the saint merely as an intermediary between him and the divine, the Hindu worships the holiness present in the saint himself. However, this takes the form of very practical requests, very similar to the prayers offered to Christian saints: help in family or business affairs, cures for sickness, even the finding of lost objects. Pilgrims seek practical miracles to deal with problems which they themselves are unable to resolve.

Despite this diversity, one city does have a particular claim

11. The ghats along the edge of the Ganges at Benares.
(Ann & Bury Peerless)

on the Hindu pilgrim's attention. This is Benares, or, to give it its correct Hindu name, Varanasi. It is also known as Kashi, 'the city of light', or more exotically, Anandavana, 'the forest of bliss'; and it has been, like Jerusalem, a holy place to more than one religion. The Buddhists long regarded it as one of their sacred sites, because Buddha came here when he was teaching his new creed, and the Jains revere it because Mahavira, the founder of their sect, lived here. The Moslem emperor Aurangzeb built his famous mosque in the middle of the holiest part of the Hindu city in a deliberate attempt to deny access to the unbelievers. But Benares today has reverted to its Hindu origins, and to the rituals centred on the river Ganges. Despite its long history as a place of Hindu worship, the temples that the pilgrims visit are all relatively modern; it was only with the decline of the Moslem empire in northern India in the early eighteenth century that the Hindus were able to rebuild their shrines, and most of them date from the late eighteenth and early nineteenth century. But in a sense the shrines are irrelevant: it is the Ganges that dominates both the city and its religious rites.

Men have worshipped the Ganges for thousands of years. Just as the Nile dominated ancient Egyptian religion, so the great river that flows from the Himalayas to the Bay of Bengal across the north Indian plain has been a focus for devotion since prehistoric times, when the early inhabitants worshipped trees and water. The Aryan invaders who conquered them in around 1200 BC brought a religion based on fire, like that of their cousins in ancient Persia; but the old and the new gradually merged and from the two Hinduism was born. Water once again became the predominant element, and Hindu myths grew up to account for the origin of the great river. One of these tells how king Sagar, lord of north India, wished to challenge the rule of Indra, king of heaven, and attempted to perform the ancient ritual of the horse sacrifice, *ashvamedha*. This involved the consecration of a specially chosen horse, which was then set free; wherever it roamed, the land became the property of the king who had consecrated it. The god Indra, fearful for his superiority, seized the horse and hid it, at which Sagar sent out his army of sons, sixty thousand strong, to lay waste the countryside and find the missing animal. In alarm, Indra called on Vishnu to defend him and the rest of the gods, and Vishnu reduced the sons of Sagar to ashes. It was only many centuries later that a devout ascetic descended from Sagar was able to obtain the release of their souls; the ashes lay unburied, and he petitioned Brahma to send a great river from heaven to cleanse the earth and free their souls. So great was the size of the river needed for the task that Shiva had to break its force with his hair, which became the peaks of the Himalayas. The cleansing power of the river endures, and all the souls of those whose ashes are placed in the river are freed from the sins accumulated in their previous existences.

Benares is also the city particularly sacred to Shiva; legend has it that it is not built on earth, but on the point of Shiva's trident, and that Shiva himself resides there for three hours each day. It is his particular realm, and he excludes from it Yama, the lord of death and of limbo, who assigns a new existence to the souls of those who have just died: hence those who die in Benares can break the cycle of reincarnation, and can escape into eternal salvation. It is death that dominates the religious rites of the city; the 'burning *ghats*', where the bodies of devout Hindus are placed on funeral pyres by the Ganges, are the most famous of the religious aspects of Benares, but it is also a place where ordinary pilgrims come in their thousands to worship and to immerse themselves in the holy river.

The rituals for pilgrims setting out on the *Kashiyatra* or journey to Benares – Hindus always refer to the city as Kashi in a religious context – were laid down in Hindu scripture and include the adoption of red robes and putting on a copper ring and a copper bracelet. In addition, pilgrims observe some or all of the practices recommended on any visit to a *tirtha*: fasting, sexual abstinence, the renunciation of luxuries, walking barefoot, are enjoined in order to cultivate the appropriate frame of mind. When the pilgrim approaches the city, he can choose between a number of different routes which lead him to the various shrines. The most esteemed is the *panchakrosi yatra*, a distance of about fifty miles, which takes five to six days to complete: 'this encompasses almost all the principal shrines...the four dhamas, seven *puris*, fifty-six manifestations of Ganesh, nine Gauris, thirteen Narsingha, sixteen Keshava (which includes Rama and Krishna, and other incarnations of Vishnu), twelve Aditya, eight Bhairava and a very large number of Shiva linga'.

At each shrine, homage and worship *(puja* and *arati)* are offered to the particular deity, while at the banks of the Ganges itself, flowers, coconuts, fruits or money may be thrown into the river as a token sacrifice. Other *yatras* take in particular sections of the city, or shrines with similar dedications, such as the *Nakshtra yatra*, which includes the shrines of the gods of the stars, planets and heavens, and which is recommended in order to ward off the effects of bad astrological omens. There are also *yatras* marked by periods of time – annual, half-yearly, monthly and so on: different bathing places are prescribed according to the month of the year.

Among the shrines of Benares, one stands out above all others, the golden temple of Vishwanath, which almost all pilgrims visit. Built by the wife of the rajah of Indore in 1777, its domes were given a golden covering in 1839: it stands in the heart of the city, approached though the narrow lanes of the old quarter. Although it is the most visited shrine, opinions vary as to its sanctity. Since 1954 the *harijans* or members of the untouchable caste have been admitted to the sanctuary; this led to the founding of a second Vishwanath temple in Benares by Swami Karapatri in protest at their presence. But at a third

Vishwanath temple in the Hindu University not only untouchables but non-Hindus are admitted to the sanctuary, and there is therefore no clear-cut attitude towards entry into the presence of the god. The central image at the Vishwanath temples is Shiva in his form as a phallus or *linga*, and elaborate ceremonies are performed there. As in most temples, these mirror the daily ritual of the god, which is that of a normal human day: the god awakes, takes his meals, and retires to bed. In the intervals, he accepts offerings from worshippers. At a humble shrine, these ceremonies may be brief and simple; at Vishwanath, they are a performance for the benefit of pilgrims, and each can last up to an hour and a half.

In addition, individual pilgrims may pay for a special act of worship, the 'greatest honour to Lord Shiva'; this is usually performed by only one priest, but in its most intense form, requires either 1,331 or 1,463 priests. In recent years the *maha rudrabhishika* was performed in 1973, and attracted considerable attention; only princes were said to be able to afford the fullest version of the ceremony.

But the chief rite practised by pilgrims to Benares is the ritual bath in the Ganges, the *Ganga snam*, which is as important a part of a pilgrimage to the city as the visit to the Golden Vishwanath temple. The *ghats* from which the bathers descend into the river are an extraordinary piece of engineering. Built in the eighteenth century for the most part, their stone embankments and steps jut into the river's fast-flowing current at a point where there is little natural rock to form a foundation; originally there were only sandy cliffs here, and the first structures were built by the Mahratta princes of the eighteenth century who drove the Moslems out of this part of India. The most popular *ghats* are the five which form the *Panch Tirtha*, a pilgrimage route in themselves. Each *ghat* has its attendants or *ghattas* who provide the necessary services for the bathers, both physical and religious; they provide soap and oils, look after the bathers' belongings, and supply the material for oblations. There is no formal rite attached to bathing, but the pilgrim usually offers his own prayers and goes from the *ghat* to worship at a nearby temple. As with the pilgrim guides at the temples, families return to the same *ghat* for generations, and build up a long-standing relationship with a family of *ghatias*. Dawn is the most auspicious time for bathing; there are also particular days when bathing acquires special merit, most notably during an eclipse of the sun or moon, when the normally crowded *ghats* become completely thronged by eager devotees.

Most famous of all, however, are the 'burning *ghats*', the great cremation sites along the river. These are not strictly places of pilgrimage, but the end of one of the many journeys through life which the Hindu believer expects to undergo. Here the funeral pyres of the believers are lit, because this is the place where Vishnu's ascetic feats and austerities earned him a boon from Shiva: that all who died in Benares or were cremated here should break free from the cycle of reincarnation. It is a variant on the story of Sagar and his horse sacrifice; but the conclusion is the same, that death or funeral rites in Benares have a special quality of release for those fortunate enough to achieve them. As a result, there are a number of hospices which cater for pilgrims who have come here to die; in this Benares is unique among the Hindu holy places. The sacred fire is guarded by a community of *harijans* or untouchables called Doms; their chief, the Dom Rajah, controls the sale of the fire to mourners, while the others maintain the *ghats*, sell wood for the pyres and organise the cremations. The cremations represent the other underlying image of Hinduism, the worship of fire: Agni, the fire-god, takes the dead to the gods, just as he takes other offerings to them when they are burnt. The fire is never allowed to go out: if no cremations are taking place, a special fire is lit instead.

Benares also has its festive occasions – not that death is a cause for mourning here, because it brings release from earthly cares – the two major ones being Shivaratri, the night of Shiva, which is celebrated throughout India at Shiva's shrines, and the full moon in November (Kartik). The Shivaratri at Benares is particularly splendid; at some temples, the ceremonies continue round the clock. This may involve a continuous recital of verses from the *Rig-Veda*, the ancient Hindu hymns, or extended versions of the daily rituals, and attracts vast numbers of pilgrims. At the full moon in November, bathing in sacred rivers is considered particularly auspicious, and since the Ganges is the holiest of all rivers, to bathe in Ganges on that day is an act of particular merit. The first bathers enter the water as early as 2.30 a.m., and the normal rituals are abbreviated so that as many pilgrims as possible can take part. The same applies to the rituals of the Golden Vishwanath temple, where special arrangements have to be made to deal with the crowds.

Benares is only one of a myriad of Hindu pilgrimage centres, in a hierarchy which is by no means clear-cut, and is much more fluid than in the more institutionalised religions such as Christianity and Islam. Spontaneous popular devotion, individual reputations and even funds from a wealthy benefactor play a much larger part in the fortunes of the smaller pilgrimage centres, and it may be that even the major shrines owe their ultimate origins to the presence of a *sadhu* (holy man) or *guru* (teacher), revered by their disciples in their lifetime, and then regarded after their death as an aspect of one of the deities, becoming mythological figures or absorbed into the worship of the god whom they particularly honoured. This process can be seen in the case of the Krishna sect which was founded by Sri Caitanya, who lived in the early sixteenth century in Bengal. A whole series of shrines are associated with his travels, and he himself is regarded by his followers as an incarnation of Krishna; the shrines of his disciples are also prominent as places of pilgrimage. The visits of such holy men to existing centres serve to reinforce the reverence in which they are held.

Within the immense diversity of Hindu tradition, there are nonetheless unifying elements, even if the vast mass of local deities and saints seem to have little to do with the higher philosophical ideas of the sages. Pilgrimage in itself is one of these unifying elements, both because it is a traditional spiritual exercise accepted by all shades of Hindu belief, and because different sects often regard the same places as holy. Although the beliefs of individuals coming to a given shrine may vary, their purpose and goal are the same.

Pilgrimage as an institution is clearly a very ancient feature of Hindu religion. The great Indian epic *Mahabharata*, written in the fourth century BC, says of pilgrimage that to stay in a *tirtha* or pilgrimage shrine is one of the highest mysteries of the sages and is even superior to sacrifices. A long section is devoted to two recitals by sages; the first gives a general list by area of the shrines and holy places of India, while the second describes the sites grouped into four geographical areas, the major divisions of India. In both cases, it seems clear that a kind of grand tour, following the movement of the sun, is implied. The lists confirm some of the points we have already made. There is an ancient association between pilgrimage goals and water, and the vast majority of the places named are either on rivers or on the coast. Some sites are chosen for their remoteness, while there are substantial groups around the sources and tributaries of the Ganges, the heartland of the Aryan civilisation from which Hinduism sprang. The *Mahabharata* recognises this: 'Just as certain limbs of the body are purer than others, so are certain places on earth more sacred – some on account of their situation, others because of their sparkling waters, and others because of the association or habitation of saintly people'. Although there are a handful of sites in the far south, the pattern that emerges represents a stage in Indian history when north-south contacts were relatively undeveloped, and when there were still large groups of non-Hindu tribes. Many of the places listed have changed in status over the centuries; minor sites figure as important centres, while the modern pilgrimage goals are either absent or noted only in passing. Part of this is perhaps due to a shift away from the worship of Brahma, whose name is associated with a number of lost sites, to Shiva, Vishnu and Krishna; no temples are specifically associated with these gods in the ancient text.

The 'grand pilgrimage' that emerges from the *Mahabharata's* often obscure text began at Pushkara in what is now western Pakistan; the route went south to the Narmada river, and then west to the coast before following the Sindhu river up into Kashmir. The sources of the Ganges and its tributaries were visited, and the general route of the Ganges was followed as far as Gaya, the greatest of the shrines. Here the pilgrim turned north again, into the Himalayan foothills, to visit more tributaries of the Ganges, and worked his way east before making his way down to the sea by way of the Ganges delta. He then followed the coastal plain, by way of Jaipur, and headed for Kanya, on the southern tip of India. The last stages took him up the west coast to a point near Goa; from there, the route to the final point, Prayaga, about two hundred miles west of Gaya, is uncertain. What we do not know, despite the considerable detail given in the epic, is whether this was a journey which anyone actually carried out: it could be a merely theoretical route, taking in the great holy places of an expanding religion, or it could be something which a handful of enthusiasts actually set out to achieve. We have no other contemporary evidence, so the question must remain open.

The next descriptions of pilgrimage routes come from the *Puranas*, texts written from perhaps the third to the fifteenth century AD. These are a diverse collection, from different regions and centuries, and it is less easy to make out an overall pattern. The purpose of pilgrimage has become more formalised, and is concerned with the performance of religious rites as well as the quest for spiritual excellence implied in the *Mahabharata*, the seeking out of holy places. Gaya, an important shrine in the *Mahabharata*, but by no means unique, appears in the *Puranas* as the most frequented and most important holy place, because it was regarded as particularly suitable for the sacrifice to deceased ancestors, one of the major ceremonies of Hindu religion. The sacred places of southern India are less prominent, perhaps because of the local bias of many of the writers; foreign visitors to India who describe Hindu pilgrimage also ignore the southern temples. The Arab traveller Alberuni, who wrote a description of India in about 1030 AD drawing on his travels there, noted the importance of pilgrimage for the Hindus, which he described as follows:

> Pilgrimages are not obligatory to the Hindus, but facultative and meritorious. A man sets off to wander to some holy region, to some much venerated idol or to some of the holy rivers. He worships in them, worships the idol, makes presents to it, recites many hymns and prayers, fasts, and gives alms to the Brahmans, the priests, and others. He shaves the hair of his head and beard, and returns home.

The pattern of modern pilgrimage in India, as with the pilgrimages of other religions, is still centred on the traditional sites. The vast majority of *tirthas* are associated with water, particularly running water; this is easily explained by the importance attached to ritual bathing in Hindu belief. A smaller group are found on hilltops, but only about a quarter of the sites are neither on water nor hills. Similarly, Shiva, Vishnu (including his avatar as Krishna) and the various aspects of the mother goddess are the deities most frequently worshipped, while Brahma hardly appears. There are regional variations, just as local saints had a particular following in medieval Europe.

Turning from the gods and their shrines to the pilgrims who

visit them, what are the purposes of their journeys? We have looked briefly at both greater and lesser goals, the highest spiritual exercises and immediate mundane needs. The ideal of a journey which enables the individual to make contact with the higher reality of the spiritual world is still very strong, visits to the holy men at the *tirthas* being part of this exploration. Major shrines have *ashrams*, the abodes of saints or ascetics who devote themselves entirely to the pursuit of *mukti*, the release from mundane life, which corresponds in many ways to the Buddhist *nirvana*, and which is the ultimate goal of all devout Hindus. Equally, rituals reinforce the feeling of belonging to a greater spiritual order, a feeling that may be particularly appealing to the lower or 'scheduled' castes, who are normally rigorously separated from the higher castes. The caste system, although tempered of its worst excesses, is still absolutely central to Hinduism. Rituals such as *mundana*, when the head is tonsured at adolescence, also mark important stages in life, and these are often the object of a pilgrimage to the appropriate shrine; for *mundana* it is usually the shrines of the mother goddess. Requests for worldly help are normally addressed to local deities, so the major, nationally recognised shrines are those to which the more spiritually-minded pilgrims make their way; the rituals they carry out are not so much the purpose of their journey as an adjunct to it. Equally, the pilgrims at the great shrines are likely to have visited other major shrines: they are wealthier and better-educated than the visitors to local shrines, who can ill afford the cost and time involved in the lengthy journeys that a major pilgrimage entails.

One shrine can be taken as an example, Badrinath in the Himalayas, in the state of Uttar Pradesh, which is one of the major national pilgrimage centres. Here there is an annual *yatra*, but because Badrinath is difficult to reach, most pilgrims visit it once in a lifetime rather than repeatedly, and the journey assumes proportionally more significance. Once at Badrinath, the pilgrim will perform certain rituals, visiting the actual shrine and taking a ritual bath. In contrast, at a lesser shrine like Hardwar, which stands on the river Ganges at the point where it flows into the north Indian plains, the visitors are much more frequent: being on the Ganges, it is one of the major sites for Hindu funerals, and it also has an annual religious fair, with particularly important ones every six and twelve years. The twelve-yearly *Kumbha* feast is the most important, and bathing in the Ganges on this occasion carries with it special religious merit. Such fairs are in themselves a major reason for pilgrimage; it is not the journey in this case, but the celebration with a host of other worshippers, which is the chief spiritual feature. However, there is also a strong commercial element, just as there used to be in the distant past at Mecca: in the early twentieth century the annual fair at Hardwar was the main horse-fair of northern India. It was therefore easy of access by both road and rail, unlike Badrinath, where a proper road was only built in the 1960s.

Modern Indian pilgrimage is a highly organised operation; interestingly, westernised Hindus visiting the great shrines often describe themselves as 'tourists' and the pilgrim industry is very similar. Pilgrimage guides are available for each state, listing the shrines to be visited, though very few, if any, of the visitors can hope to reach all of them: the guide for Nepal in 1954 listed no fewer than 2,733 holy places. The origin of each is discussed; miracles performed there are noted, as are the merits to be gained. Pilgrimages are organised by official tour guides or *pandas*, who act as agents, and make the necessary travel arrangements. At the shrines themselves, the hostels are often divided by region and by caste, although in theory they are open to all. At the shrines themselves, there may be officials whose duty it is to look after pilgrims from a given region; the *pandas* at Hardwar, known as *purohits*, keep very detailed records of pilgrims, each family specialising in pilgrims from a given caste

12. Pilgrims performing puja at Allahabad, at the site where the Kumbha mela is held.
(Ann & Bury Peerless)

13. Pilgrims at a Hindu festival at Duruthu Perahera.
(Ann & Bury Peerless)

and area. As a result, their records are of considerable genealogical interest, and they are able to 'place' a newcomer with little difficulty, as well as identifying potential pilgrims, because each visitor tells the *purohit* about as many of his relatives on his father's side as he can recall. This process has been extended until some of the *purohits* go out regularly in search of clients, and organise tours in the same way as the *pandas*. The relationship between the *purohit* and his client is not simply for the duration for one pilgrimage. The *purohits* are often experts on other shrines, and will advise on a client's subsequent pilgrimages. The relationship may also extend for generations, the same pilgrims or *jajmans* using the services of a *purohit* family on a regular basis.

Furthermore, the actual shrines which attract pilgrims may be set up almost as commercial enterprises, relying as they do on offerings from visitors rather than on any centralised system. There is no overall hierarchy or organisation within Hindu religion, and hence the enthusiasm of a single devotee can result in the establishment of a new place of worship, which may well become a recognised place of pilgrimage in a relatively short time. The major pilgrimage site in West Bengal, Tarakeswar, dates from about 1730, when the presence of a particularly revered holy man was said to have led the god Shiva to reveal himself in the form of a black stone representing his *linga*. The stone was identified because the prize cow of a local herdsman used to go to it and release her milk onto it. This chain of events was completed by a miraculous cure, and the local ruler arranged for the building of a temple to Shiva. The holy man, Maya Giri, had come to the district to preach the cult of Shiva, so he was appointed first keeper of the temple, and thus fulfilled his mission. Shiva was said to have appeared as the god Taraknatha, who is thus the local deity; his particular attribute is the performance of miracles and the granting of earthly desires rather than the bestowing of other-worldly merits, and he represents the god's direct involvement with creation.

Taking Tarakeswar as an example, the actual organisation of a pilgrimage temple works on these lines. The temple was originally owned by the religious community (*matha*) there, of which the *mahanta* is the head; although this changed in 1925, the *mahanta* is the head of the temple organisation, both in religious and administrative matters. The functions of the temple include the provision of religious education, the offering of hospitality to any visiting *sannyasi* or ascetic, and the provision of charity in various forms. As a result, it has always been very much a secular organisation as well as a place of worship, very similar to the great landowning monasteries of medieval Europe: despite his vows as a *sannyasi*, the *mahanta* is just as much involved in the secular world as a medieval abbot, with financial and political obligations. He plays little part in the day-to-day reception of pilgrims, but an ambitious *mahanta* may well seek to promote 'his' pilgrimage. At Tarakeswar, one of the three major annual festivals, the fair in the month of Sravana, seems to have been deliberately promoted by a *mahanta*, Satisacandra Giri, who held office from 1892-1925. The main ceremony performed by pilgrims is the carrying of water from the Ganges to Tarakeswar, and the festival was apparently designed to attract the support of a particular wealthy group within the Bengali community, the Marwaris, for whom the Sravana fair is the chief religious event of the year. What is certain is that the festival is not recorded in 1912 or earlier, and the rite of carrying water from the Ganges to the shrine, where it is poured over the sacred stone, seems to have been copied from a temple in Bihar.

The daily ritual at the temple centres round the image of Baba Taraknatha, and begins at 4 a.m., when the statue is oiled, bathed and decorated before being covered; this ceremony is not open to the pilgrims, who are admitted at 6 a.m. The first public ceremony is at 9 a.m., when the statue is uncovered, bathed and dried before the recital of praises and prayers by the various priestly families. This is followed by the afternoon worship at 4 p.m., when the same opening ritual is performed, but it is followed by *arati* – defined as 'the circular waving of objects, especially fire, before the deity' and the offering of cannabis and tobacco to the god. After the doors are closed, food is also offered by the priests, and this is later distributed to the pilgrims in return for a payment; these payments are one of the chief resources of the temple. The evening ceremony is similar; afterwards, behind closed doors, the decoration applied at dawn is removed and the deity is offered a bed. The temple is then closed to pilgrims.

The major festivals, other than the Sravana fair, are the Gajan, a widespread festival in Bengal, and the Shivaratri or 'night of Shiva'. At the Gajan festival, the devout pilgrim takes a temporary vow of asceticism, and joins the *sannyasis*; he wears ochre robes, eats only vegetarian foods, refrains from sexual contact, and gives himself up to devotions and prayers. All caste associations are renounced, and the temporary *sannyasi* is regarded as belonging to the 'clan of Shiva' only. This initiation may be for the whole month in which the festival falls, or for a few days only, during the fair at the end of the month. The fair lasts ten days and pilgrims from different regions attend on specified days, in order to ease the pressure caused by the large numbers. The last four days have special rites, including offerings to the god: and on the last day, the Bengali New Year's Day, the *sannyasis* who have sworn temporary vows return to ordinary life, removing their ochre robes and performing the appropriate rituals.

At the daily services and major festivals, the pilgrim is largely an onlooker; but he can also perform personal devotions if he so wishes. There is one particular practice peculiar to Tarakeswar, the fast known as *dharna*, when the pilgrim sleeps on the marble floor in the temple precinct and takes no food for five days, awaiting instructions from the god in a dream: if he carries out these instructions successfully, his desire – usually a cure from a serious illness – will be granted. If the dream does not occur, most pilgrims give up after five days. This is a relatively unusual practice, though three or four pilgrims on any given day will probably be undertaking *dharna*. The usual rituals of individual pilgrims consist of offering worship *(puja)*, simply seeing the deity *(darsana)*, partaking of the food offered to him *(prasada)* or circling the temple in a clockwise direction *(pradaksina)*.

The diversity of Hindu practice and belief make it difficult to generalise about pilgrimage practices. The four rituals just outlined are typical ways in which a pilgrim may worship, but the details and emphasis will vary widely. By looking at a range of temples, we can gain some kind of overall impression, even if it only confirms the lack of a standard, general ritual such as is found in other religions with a more formal structure.

Navadvip, on the Ganges in western Bengal, owes its fame to Sri Caitanya, whom we have already mentioned, the founder of a Hindu revival known as the Gaudiya Vaisnava cult. His followers believe him to be one of the avatars or incarnations of Krishna; born at Navadvip in 1486, the son of a Brahman scholar, he first became a Brahman himself, teaching students in his own school in a city which was already famous for its learning. After his father's death and funeral at Gaya, Caitanya fell into a state of religious ecstasy, which took the form of a passionate devotion to Krishna. He settled in Puri, in Orissa, where he taught and inspired followers until his death in 1533. A mystical teacher's influence does not often survive his own lifetime, but his followers succeeded in both deriving a system from his teachings and forming an organised cult. Today Caitanya is worshipped at Navadvip as an avatar of Krishna, with all the attributes of Krishna's particular cult. The main ritual at the temples is the chanting of Krishna's praises *(kirtana)*, although the practice of treating the god as a living being with a daily round of actions corresponding to the human one – getting up, taking meals, bathing and going to bed – is found here too. Less usual is the cult of relics, both of objects belonging to Caitanya himself and of items belonging to his disciples. The Vaisnava cult is also unusual in having an international aspect, in the shape of the International Society for Krishna Consciousness, which makes Navadvip a place of international pilgrimage; there is an *ashram* or religious centre especially set aside for foreigners. A pilgrim's visit, if he is a Vaisnava, will centre on the places associated with Caitanya, and in this it is closer to Christian pilgrimage sites, with their emphasis on mementoes of the saints, than to other Hindu temple complexes. Other pilgrims are orthodox Hindus, because the goddess Sakti has an important shrine here, and the presence of the Ganges is always a magnet for those who wish to take their ritual bath in the holy river; although the Vaisnava beliefs are in many ways at variance with those of orthodox Hinduism, the underlying similarities allow the two to coexist in harmony, and in many cases the same deity is revered for different reasons. The bulk of the pilgrims come from the surrounding countryside, and in this sense it is a largely local, if unusual, pilgrimage centre.

The second of our sample of Hindu shrines, and the most spectacular in architectural terms, is that of Jagannath at Puri in Orissa, on the north-eastern coast of the Bay of Bengal. Puri was one of the places where Caitanya lived for a time, and Caitanya's followers regard it with especial reverence because of the connection with their leader. For the majority of Hindus, its fame is as the home of the image of Krishna known as Jagannath. This is said to contain the bones of Krishna, and to have been made by the god Vishvakarman, who, because he was interrupted in his work, left it without hands or feet. Brahma, at the request of the local ruler, finished the image and gave it eyes and a soul. At the climax of the annual festival in Jagannath's honour, pilgrims pull the image to the nearby sacred lake on a specially constructed chariot. There was a myth that ardent worshippers flung themselves under its wheels, believing that to die in this fashion ensured instant entry into heaven; but in fact such deaths were usually accidental. If such an accident occurred, the procession was stopped, and a ritual purification was carried out. Once again we are confronted with the duality of Hindu worship: extreme spirituality combined with a highly physical approach. On the one hand, we have pilgrims who retrace the steps of the great teachers and holy men, engaged in meditation and spiritual exercises; on the other, we have the uncontrolled physical ecstasy of the enthusiast.

The massive stone temple at Puri rises to over two hundred feet; at its top are Vishnu's sacred wheel and flag. It is a worthy marker of one of the four great dhamas of Hindu tradition. The temple was built in the twelfth century by the kings of Orissa, who later ritually dedicated their lands to Jagannath. But Puri was already an ancient religious site; it was a Buddhist shrine in the fifth century BC, and the Jagannath temple may stand on the site of a temple which contained one of Buddha's teeth. Puri continued to be a holy place with the re-emergence of Hinduism in the fifth century AD; even after a thousand years of Buddhism, the ancient traditions of Jagannath, were remembered and revived. The town contains ancient monastic houses, which can trace their existence back to the eighth century AD. The legend of the revival has striking echoes of the rediscovery of sacred relics elsewhere. The king of Orissa enquired of the local scholars and priests where he might find Jagannath, 'lord of the kings of Orissa', and was told that the images from Puri had been taken to a village in western Orissa. After some difficulty, he found the images (of Jagannath and his two companions Balbhadra and Subhadra), but they were so worn with age that he decided to renew them. However the priests who alone could carry out the task had also fled, and were only found after a further search: Hindu priesthood was, and still is, hereditary, and it was therefore essential that the right men were found. The priests were re-established at Puri and the new images were installed. The temple was unusual in its political importance: patronage of the temple by the kings of Orissa was a consistent feature of its history, and even the Moslems, who were generally hostile to Hindu shrines because they were a focus for political opposition, reinstated the pilgrimage in 1735 after a long period of anarchy, largely because the taxes from pilgrims were so lucrative. When the East India Company's troops under Lt Col Campbell conquered Orissa in 1803, strict instructions were given that the temple should not be harmed, and that the Brahmans there were to be put under the army's protection to ensure their safety.

The million or so pilgrims who visit Puri each year almost all use the services of the priests, who act as pilgrim guides, the *pandas* or *puja pandas* mentioned earlier. Each *puja panda* has his own area of the country to look after; if there is a shortage of pilgrims, he or his agent may visit the area in question to arrange for pilgrimages. The *puja panda* instructs the pilgrim in the rituals of the temple and arranges for the purchase of flowers, food and lights which are offered to the god; the pilgrims prostrate themselves before the images. Normally respect or *darshan* is paid to the gods during the hours when the temple is open, but it is possible, on paying a fee, to make a private visit to the shrine; other symbols of devotion are the placing of a banner or name-plate in the temple to record a visit or as thanks for a successful prayer.

The rituals at Puri are particularly extensive; five main services marking the events of the god's day are divided into sixteen stages, with appropriate chants and hymns, but for the ordinary pilgrim it is his or her personal contact with the deity that is important. There are separate *pujas* or forms of worship for each of the three gods, and for the three lesser gods in the sanctuary, so that the temple is continuously busy, and pilgrims often have to content themselves with a distant bow towards the sanctuary rather than a full length prostration before the god. The great festival of Jagannath is in June or July, in the Hindu month Ashadha, when the god is put on a specially-made carriage drawn by the *puja pandas*, and is taken to a nearby lake for a ritual bath; this naturally attracts a very large number of pilgrims.

Our third and last shrine is that at Gaya, in Bihar, on the edge of the Ganges plain. Again, this is an ancient site, but it is remarkable for keeping both Buddhist and Hindu traditions alive: there are effectively two cities, Hindu Gaya and Bodh (or Buddhist) Gaya, six miles apart. Bodh Gaya, visited by many famous Buddhist pilgrims, now co-exists peacefully with the Hindu shrine, and many Hindus pay their respects to Buddha, as well as joining in the festival in April or May which marks the day of Buddha's enlightenment under the Bodhi tree there. The Buddhist shrine dates from Buddha's own time, the fifth century BC, and much of it was built by the devout Buddhist emperor Asoka in the third century BC. The Hindu complex is much later, dating from AD 1000 onwards; around 1060, a local ruler boasts in an inscription of raising it from a village to the equal of Amravati, a city famed for its splendour. In the thirteenth century, a temple to the sun-god was built, possibly under the influence of priests from Persia; this still exists, and is one of the oldest of the Gayan shrines. Another temple is actually dedicated to a great temple builder, the Mahratta queen Ahilya Bai, who raised the temple of Vishnu and a great bathing *ghat* on the river Phalgu, which flows through the town; she also built temples at Benares, and is now worshipped in her own shrine.

In addition to the standard forms of worship we have already discussed in relation to other shrines, Gaya is noteworthy for its sacred recitations, or *sankirtana*, which take place every evening, and once a month a whole day and night are devoted to a continuous performance. Although pilgrims may join in, this is essentially a performance by a specialist group at which the pilgrim is a spectator. Much more important, and the main reason for pilgrimage to Gaya, is the performance of *shraddha* or sacrifice in honour of one's ancestors. It is an extremely ancient tradition, going back two thousand years; the early *Puranas* or sacred books mention it, and give detailed instructions for its performance. As with any other Hindu pilgrimage, a pilgrim who sets out to perform *shraddha* at Gaya must do so in the right spirit; austerity and abstinence are prescribed, and on arrival at Gaya, he must fast for a day before donning the ritual white garments required for the sacrifice. He offers flowers and coins at the feet of the priests, and then embarks on the complicated series of water offerings, for which one of the assistant priests acts as a guide; these are carried out in the river Phalgu, to the accompaniment of readings from the ritual book. The major gods and the great sages are honoured first, followed by the god of death, Yama, who is asked to be merciful to the ancestors of the pilgrim. Finally, offerings are made to bring peace to the ancestors themselves. This ritual is followed on the next day by offerings of rice cake (*pinda*), made to each ancestor individually and to the gods, in a complex series of symbolic acts, accompanied again by recitals, this time of hymns from the *Rig-Veda*. The sacrificer then visits a number of the sacred sites in Gaya and makes further offerings; the rite concludes with a ceremony in which the priest of the temple – in return for suitable gifts – declares, as representative of the gods and ancestors, that he is satisfied with the *shraddha*.

Shraddha pilgrims come for a variety of reasons; they wish to express their devotion to the deceased; they regard the ritual as something which will bring peace and prosperity to their family; and they even use it as a means of warding off their fear of ghosts and of spirits. *Shraddha* is one of the most extensive of all pilgrimage rituals, representing the so-called 'great tradition' of Hinduism at its best; but its sheer complexity makes it impossible for very large numbers of pilgrims to carry it out, and its popularity has declined in favour of less onerous forms of worship.

Each region has its particular style of pilgrimage, just as the same gods are revered in different *avatars*. At Pandharpur, near Bombay, the Mahrattas worship Vishnu under the name of Vithoba, and his great festivals coincide with two great fairs, at which the horse-dealers of the region gather. But the pilgrims far outnumber the merchants, and the pilgrimage is a highly organised one. Each village brings its relics in procession to the temple, and within each such group the pilgrims are organised into sections which meet throughout the rest of the year. The great feature of Mahratta pilgrimages is their music; the groups have singers, drummers and cymbal-players, and know hundreds of hymns by heart. There is an entire genre of Mahratta poetry devoted to pilgrimage songs, and the relic carried by the procession is a little plaque engraved with the footprints of the local poet-saint who began their particular pilgrimage. Through his songs, he is still at the heart of their journey, which is not an ascetic experience like that of the holy men of Hinduism, but a pilgrimage undertaken out of devotion to the god. It is a popular, enthusiastic occasion, which, as elsewhere, does not necessarily meet with the approval of the temple priests.

One of the great pilgrimage places on the Ganges, recognised by both the *Mahabharata* and the *Puranas* as one of the holiest, if not the holiest, sites in India is Prayaga, known to the British as Allahabad, upstream from Gaya at the point where the Ganges and the Jumna meet. The annual pilgrimage, fair or *Magh mela* is a considerable attraction; it is held at the time regarded as most auspicious for bathing, in January and February. Every twelve years, however, there is a particular astrological conjunction, and if, as in 1989, this coincides with a lunar eclipse, the time is held to be especially holy. The 1989

Kumbha mela, as the twelve-yearly celebration is called, attracted fifteen million pilgrims to Prayaga, making it one of the largest gatherings the world has ever seen, and far outstripping the annual pilgrimage to Mecca. It acts as a focal point for the diversity of Hindu tradition, with representatives from the great Hindu monastic centres gathering there, as well as the many different kinds of holy men, the *sadhus* who perform extraordinary vows and the militaristic members of the *akhadas*, trained in the martial arts. The main ritual is of course bathing in Ganges: at the peak of the festivities six hundred thousand people an hour entered the river. A vast encampment, covering five and a half square miles, was set up for the pilgrims; the atmosphere was half that of a medieval pageant, as the *mahantas* passed in their baroque gilded bullock-carts, garlanded in the traditional fashion, and the naked, ash-smeared *sadhus* performed their strange feats, and half that of a vast modern fairground, with neon-lit displays by night and groups of entertainers by day. Sometimes the two merged imperceptibly: on the one hand, there were the religious minstrels, performers in a tradition going back for centuries, whose recitals of epics and songs in praise of the deities were rewarded by alms from the *sadhus* themselves, while on the other hand, as one of the religious leaders observed, there were *sadhus* whose acts belonged more to the theatre than to the world of ascetic yoga. On a more serious level, the saffron-robed learned *sadhus* expounded Hindu doctrine to the pilgrims and held conferences on Hindu theology, so that the fair functioned as a meeting-place for serious religious discussion while the extraordinary throngs of pilgrims swarmed to and from the sacred river.

The localised nature of Hindu worship makes it the most diverse of the great religions. Yet behind its diversity, the same central beliefs are constant: the idea of reincarnation and the search for spiritual improvement as a way out of the endless cycle of death and rebirth, the concept of the gods as active forces in daily life, the value of pilgrimage as a religious exercise – all these transcend local custom and practice. To them one could add the idea of great rivers as sacred, and the ordinary believer's concept of the images of the gods as the actual seats of divinity, 'the incarnations which Vishnu and others have assumed to receive worship from mortal beings'. All these elements go towards the shaping of the Hindu ideal of pilgrimage, which is one of the main forces which bind Hinduism together. It cuts across the divisions of caste – a barrier which has always puzzled and concerned observers from other civilisations, but which is central to Hindu thought. Above all, Hindu pilgrimage makes considerable demands on the individual. As a recent Hindu writer puts it:

> The mystic potency of a sacred stream may confer a minor benefit on the person who immerses himself in its holy waters, without even believing in its value. But to attain the full spiritual advantages of a *yatra*, it must be commenced with a definite purpose and in the full faith that the journey, when completed in the proper frame of mind and without any lapse of the austerities prescribed, will yield the highest unworldly advantage.... Life affords numerous opportunities for the ascent to spiritual perfection, which will end [the cycle of birth and] re-birth. One of such opportunities is furnished by the discipline of pilgrimage which is not an end in itself but only one of the means to the highest ends.

CHAPTER FIVE

Buddhist pilgrimage: pilgrimage as quest

The ultimate pilgrimage in Buddhist belief is the spiritual journey, through meditation, 'to discover the Buddha nature within oneself'. But the search for images and relics of Buddha is regarded as an important first step in the path to enlightenment, and Buddha himself encouraged the development of a cult of relics when, on his deathbed, he ordered his disciple Ananda to cremate his body and enshrine it in *stupas* or cairns. His ashes were divided among eight such *stupas*; a ninth contained his alms bowl and another was created to house the remains of the funeral pyre. These *stupas* acted as the focal points for Buddhist worship for two hundred years, from the death of Buddha in the late fifth century BC until the time of emperor Asoka, in the late third century BC.

Until Asoka's time, Buddhism was a relatively obscure and strict sect; his conversion led to it becoming a religion with a mass following, and in some respects, to a relaxation of the original standards demanded by Buddha of his followers. Asoka himself, who was ruler of the Punjab and the upper Ganges valley, seems to have been converted as the result of a *dharmayatra* or journey in search of the truth, to none other than Gaya, whose Hindu pilgrimages we have just described. It was at Gaya, or more correctly Bodh Gaya (Buddhist Gaya) that Buddha attained enlightenment under the sacred Bodhi tree, a descendant of which is still the focal point of the Buddhist temple there. Asoka's pilgrimage seems to be the first record of

14. The *stupa* or tower containing a relic of the Buddha at Sarnath, the site where the Buddha preached for the first time. (Ann & Bury Peerless)

such an expedition, and marks both the expansion of the faith and the introduction of the popular customs of the older Hindu religion into Buddhism. We know about Asoka's journeys from the book-inscriptions of his edicts, thirty-five of which still survive. It was he who rediscovered Buddha's birthplace outside Kapilavastu, the town to the north of Benares where Buddha's father was the ruler; Asoka marked the site with a stone pillar for the benefit of future pilgrims. He also visited the *stupa* which held the ashes of Konakamana, an earlier teacher whose follower Buddha claimed to be. Asoka is said to have taken the relics of Buddha from the ten *stupas* which held them and to have redistributed them in minute portions between eighty-four thousand new *stupas*; the number is obviously mythical, but Asoka undoubtedly spread the influence of Buddhism throughout his empire, and created numerous new sacred sites. A tradition, which belongs to the period after pilgrimage had become an established Buddhist practice, records that Buddha told Ananda that there were four places which should be seen by 'every son of a good family of believers: the place where Buddha was born [Kapilavastu]; the place where he obtained enlightenment [Bodh Gaya]; the place where the kingdom of doctrine was established by him [Sarnath]; the place where Buddha entered into total extinction [Kushinagara]'.

The great period of Buddhism in India lasted until the fifth century AD, when it was gradually swept aside by a revived Hindu religion which had absorbed many of the Buddhist teachings. As a result the pilgrimage sites intimately associated with Buddha became difficult of access: Kapilavastu, his birthplace, Sarnath near Benares where he preached for the first time and Kushinagara where he attained the state of 'nirvana', were all more or less abandoned as Buddhist religious centres, and only Bodh Gaya, the place where his mission began, retained its original importance. As Buddhism spread outwards from India, so new pilgrimage sites centred on real or imagined relics of Buddha were established. A tradition grew up that Buddha had supernaturally visited these distant lands, leaving his footprints imprinted on rocks as far afield as the Punjab and Adam's Peak in Ceylon. Ceylon also boasted one of the most famous of all relics, Buddha's tooth, enshrined in the temple at Kandy. These real or fabled traces of the Buddha served as focal points for the newly established religion.

Chinese pilgrimage

Just as Christian pilgrims from Europe sought out the homeland of their Messiah, so the Buddhists from China regarded India as a kind of Holy Land. Buddhism first gained a foothold in China around 65 AD, but did not become a major religion there until the end of the Han dynasty, in the third century AD. The first Buddhist travellers from the 'middle kingdom' seem to have reached India about this time; the first to leave a record of his wanderings was Fa-Hsien, whose *Records of Buddhist Countries* begin in 400 AD. His purpose, like most Chinese pilgrims to India, was to seek out Buddhist writings in order to establish the true teachings of the Buddha. Good copies of the central texts of Buddhism were rare, and many of the teachings had become distorted in translation. The first stages of Fa-Hsien's journey took him in a wide circle across central Asia and then down into north-east India. Once in India, he began to record the relics of Buddha which he encounters: his alms bowl at Peshawar, his skull, kept at Hidda under strict security:

> The king of the country profoundly reverences the skull-bone. Fearing lest some one should steal it, he appoints eight men of the first families of the country, each man having a seal to seal [the door] for its safe keeping. In the morning, the eight men having come, each one inspects his seal, and then they open the door. The door being opened, using scented water, they wash their hands and bring out the skull-bone of Buddha.

They place it outside the *vihâra* on a high throne; taking a circular stand of the seven precious substances, the stand is placed below [it], and a glass bell as a cover over it. All these are adorned with pearls and gems. The bone is of a yellowish-white colour, four inches across and raised in the middle. Each day after its exit men of the *vihâra* at once mount a high tower, beat a large drum, blow the conch, and sound the cymbal. Hearing these, the king goes to the *vihâra* to offer flowers and incense. The offerings finished, each one in order puts it on his head [worships it] and departs. Entering by the east door and leaving by the west, the king every morning thus offers and worships, after which he attends to state affairs.

Fa-Hsien also recorded legends about the life of Buddha. He found Kapilavastu, Buddha's birthplace, 'like a great desert; you seldom meet any people on the roads for fear of the white elephants and the lions', and the palace of Buddha's father was in ruins. Yet he was able to record the reasons for each of the numerous towers which marked episodes in Buddha's life. By contrast, he found a flourishing community of priests at Patna, but Bodh Gaya itself was 'desolate and desert', though there were three congregations of priests at the temple itself. The general picture he paints is of an impoverished country where Buddhism survived as a shadow of its former self; he had considerable trouble in finding the sacred books which he wanted. His journey lasted eleven years, and he passed through almost thirty kingdoms before he finally sailed for China, which he reached after a dangerous voyage by way of Java.

Tripitaka is perhaps the most familiar of the great Chinese Buddhist pilgrims to western readers because of his appearance in legendary form in the novel *Monkey*. Behind this legendary figure lies a real historical person, Hsuan-Tsang, not merely a great traveller but a much-respected teacher and scholar. His journey to India, which began when he was 27, in 629 AD, was undertaken in search of new teachers and writings in the land where Buddha himself had lived; as in Fa-Hsien's case, it was an attempt to reach the authentic tradition of Buddhist philosophy. But Tripitaka was also particularly anxious to find a personal creed among the many sects and divergences of theory which he himself could confidently teach. His expertise in the Chinese Buddhist traditions was already famous, but had only led him personally to doubts and indecision. Hence his journey was very much a spiritual quest, rather than a desire simply to revere the memory of Buddha, and to worship and meditate at the places where he had taught and lived.

After an initial disaster when he lost the contents of his water flask and went thirsty for several days, his journey out of China and across the Himalayas was relatively easy. The ruler of one of the kingdoms bordering China, Turfan, was so impressed by Tripitaka that he gave him gold, silver and silk and a large escort. On his way, he met many Buddhists of varying sects, in particular those of the Hinayana, who did not share his more orthodox belief, as a follower of the Mahayana, that the world is an illusion; the followers of the Hinayana believed that it had a real existence. He travelled through Afghanistan, and entered India near Peshawar. His journey now became a gradual progress from monastery to monastery, and from teacher to teacher, learning from and disputing with each in terms of his own particular sect's beliefs, something at which Tripitaka was especially adept. He began to collect Buddhist books unknown in China, or of which no copies were available there. After staying for a time in Kashmir and the Punjab, he travelled down the Ganges valley to Bodh Gaya and Benares, the area where Buddha had lived. His reputation was already considerable, because while he was at Bodh Gaya monks from Nalanda, the home of the leading teacher of the Idealist School of Buddhists, Silabhadra, came to take him to their master. It was in effect a university, and here Tripitaka studied for five years, finding in particular the *Yoga Sastra*, a text which was only partly known in China; he heard Silabhadra's course of lectures on it three

15. The Buddhist temple at Bodh Gaya, the place where the Buddha received enlightenment. (Ann & Bury Peerless)

times. After these studies, he set out for Ceylon, where, he believed, he would find masters both of primitive Buddhism and of the Idealist School; but when he reached the port in southern India where he was to embark, he met a party of monks who had just fled the country because civil war had broken out. He therefore returned by the west coast to Nalanda, where he spent several years lecturing and debating, as well as meeting new teachers such as the hermit Jayasina who lived in the forest near by. He had already decided to return to China when he was summoned by the king of Assam and then by the king of the region around Cawnpore in order to convert them and their subjects to the Mahayana form of Buddhism, which, according to his biographer, he successfully did before he returned to China by way of Kashgar. His journey had lasted sixteen years; it had been in turn a pilgrimage, a quest for knowledge, and a missionary venture.

The great age of Buddhism in China came to an end in the ninth century, when, as in India, it was supplanted by a religion which blended both old and new traditions, Taoism. Taoism took many of its spiritual concepts from Buddhism, but its religious practices were rooted in the earlier Chinese religion. One practical aspect, however, which Taoism seems to owe to Buddhism is the idea of pilgrimage. The modern Chinese pilgrimage sites, until the communists came to power in 1949 were dominated by the 'sacred five', the five great mountain sanctuaries of Taoist belief, and there were in addition four major Buddhist mountain sites which survived. The Buddhist sites were at Wu-tai, P'ou-t'o, O-mei and Chiu-hua. Each had its own deity, a Bodhisattva or 'future Buddha', and each corresponded to one of the four elements – air, water, fire and earth respectively – as well as to one of the four points of the compass. The most important was Mount Wu-tai, sacred to Manjusri, the Bodhisattva who was said to have conquered Yama, the god of death. Under the T'ang dynasty, it was one of the greatest pilgrimage sites in Asia, visited by pilgrims not only from China but from India, Tibet and Japan.

One of the pilgrims who came from Japan was a monk called Ennin; the journal he wrote on his pilgrimage in the middle of the ninth century AD has survived. He came to China as a diplomat, on an embassy to the T'ang emperor, but stayed behind without permission in order to study Buddhism. He therefore had to make his pilgrimage as a poor monk, begging his way and taking advantage of the hospitality offered by the monasteries along the route. Pilgrims were not always welcome, even though it was accepted that it was a religious duty to entertain them, but despite some awkward moments, Ennin found that in general travel was not difficult, and he commented admiringly on the hospices which had been specially built in the more sparsely populated areas for the benefit of pilgrims. Wu-tai was a spectacular site, and when Ennin visited it in 840, he admired not only the five terraces, but the flowers and pine-trees which covered the mountain. He was particularly impressed, as he made his way round the five terraces, paying homage at each of the many shrines, by the relics of Buddha at the main monastery, and by the revolving bookcase, containing a large number of volumes, housed in a nearby tower; a pilgrim who made it revolve once earned as much merit as by reading all the volumes it contained.

In the late thirteenth century, when the Mongols invaded China, Wu-tai became a particular centre for the Tibetan form of Buddhism, which the Mongols favoured, and in which Manjusri is one of the chief deities. For many centuries the two traditions of Buddhism co-existed at Mount Wu-tai, but under the Ch'ing dynasty, from 1644 onwards, the Tibetan tradition began to predominate, and it became the holiest site of the Mongol Buddhists.

At the mountain site of O-mei, P'ou-hien or Samantabdhadra is worshipped, in popular belief a Bodhisattva who came from

India on a white elephant to take up residence as the deity who protects O-mei; like Manjusri, he is an important figure in Tibetan Buddhism. Mount O-mei is in the west of China, far from the main Chinese cities, but relatively close to the Tibetan border: yet until the Second World War, it was one of the major pilgrimage sites in the country. The chief monastery, on the lower slopes of the mountain, was the 'monastery of ten thousand years', which contained a huge bronze statue, twenty-four feet high, of P'ou-hien, dating from the tenth century. The pilgrims rubbed their hands on the feet and trunk of the elephant, or placed money or other objects on it, which then became luck-bearing tokens. A much more remarkable custom was the bringing of small statues of the gods to O-mei, which were left for a time in niches in the walls of the sanctuary, to be fetched on a subsequent journey, so that they could acquire magical power by being near the deity. The whole monastery was destroyed during the war, and rebuilt shortly before being closed by the communists. Other monasteries stood on a plateau three thousand feet below the peak itself, and housed pilgrims who hoped to see the 'glory of Buddha', a miraculous light which sometimes appeared at night among the clouds shrouding the valley below.

The Zen monastery of Mount P'ou-t'o is sacred to Kuan-yin, the goddess of compassion; in 847 AD, a monk had a vision of her in a grotto on the island, and, as with visions of the Virgin Mary in Europe, the island at once became a pilgrimage site. It was sacked in 1665 by Dutch raiders, but the monasteries were rebuilt by the emperor. In 1949, there were about a thousand monks in the hundred or so monasteries; the annual festival in honour of Kuan-yin, on the nineteenth day of the second lunar month, was celebrated by ceremonies in all the monasteries, and attracted large numbers of pilgrims.

Ordinary pilgrims did not take part in the Taoist pilgrimages to the five sacred mountains until after the Buddhist period, but in ancient China, ritual pilgrimage was one of the sacred duties of the emperor. As with the Buddhist sites, the five sacred mountains represented to the Taoist worshipper the four cardinal points of the compass, and the centre, thus marking out the boundaries of the 'Middle Kingdom', the Chinese name for the country, as well as conforming to the idea of sacred harmony. The most solemn of all sacrifices was that called *fong chan*, which could only be carried out by the emperor on a pilgrimage to Mount T'ai: the ritual was carried out at the peak and foot of the mountain. It was so awe-inspiring that only five emperors ever carried it out, in 110 BC, 56 AD, 666 AD, 725 AD and 1008 AD, and inscriptions recorded each occasion, emphasising its grandeur: in 725 Hiuan-tsong declared that he had summoned his six imperial armies for the event. After the Buddhists had introduced the idea of popular pilgrimage, Mount T'ai became one of the objects of such journeys, but instead of the Emperor of the Eastern Peak, whom the emperors had worshipped, the pilgrims now revered Pi-hia-yuan-Kuin, 'the princess of the rainbow clouds', his daughter.

Pilgrimage was called by the Chinese 'journeying to a mountain and offering incense', a phrase which underlines the emphasis on mountain shrines. It was regarded as a way of acquiring spiritual merit, and it was generally a well-organised expedition rather than a solitary journey. Pilgrims would form a temporary society, called 'an association for burning incense', and would invite others to join them. A kind of savings bank would be set up, into which the participants would make payments at intervals until there were sufficient funds for the journey, because in China pilgrims did not beg. The usual time for setting out was the Chinese New Year, and the group would carry with them a banner inscribed with their place of origin. Pilgrimage was generally taken seriously, and strict rules of behaviour were observed: there was no idle gossip on the way, and pilgrims were expected to abstain from meat and sexual

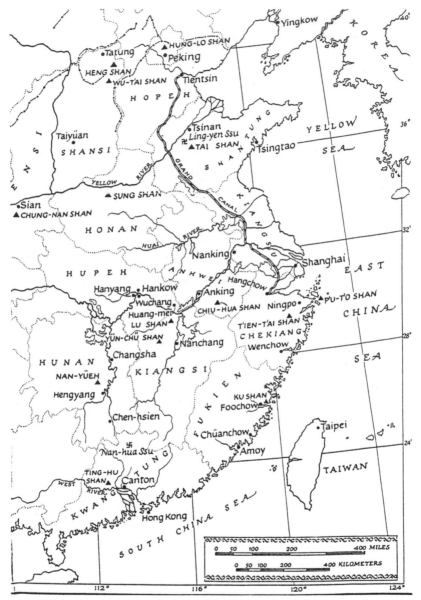

17. The major shrines of China (*shan* = mountain)
Reproduced from Holmes Welch, *The Practice of Chinese Buddhism*, by permission of Harvard University Press

relations. Vegetarianism was enforced at Mount P'ou-t'o by a rule that no animal could be killed there. When pilgrims stopped at a monastery, they would be accommodated in separate dormitories for men and women, and there would be no charge; how much they gave was up to each pilgrim, but it was understood that the more generous the donation, the greater the spiritual merit acquired. At the Fu-hu Ssu temple on O-mei in the high season (from May to September) several hundred pilgrims might be guests each day, looked after by the younger monks. However, there was no obligation on monasteries to open their doors to pilgrims, and many of the stricter houses actually discouraged visitors, because their presence detracted from the religious atmosphere. Pilgrimage to major shrines was seasonal, related to important dates in the calendars of the temples, and the round of shrines at one of the four sacred mountains, if carried out in minute detail, could last for weeks rather than days.

A different but equally important type of pilgrimage was that carried out by Buddhist monks, usually after the period when they had perfected their knowledge of the monastic rules. This was *ts'an fang* or 'travelling to every quarter of the country'. It was similar to the practices of some Hindu holy men or to the itinerant friars in medieval Europe, and there was a parallel in Amida Buddhism in Japan. In part, it was designed to accustom the monk to hardship and to wean him from any dependence on creature comforts, because there was no certainty that he would find lodging, and he would have little or no money to pay for a room. The other objectives of this time of travel were to visit the four Buddhist sacred mountains and their monasteries, and the great public monasteries elsewhere. At these public monasteries, wandering monks could stay as long as they wished, attending lectures or meditating, until they were ready to depart.

Monks going to the sacred mountains might also carry out

physical penances, similar to those found in Tibet, such as prostrating themselves by touching their head on the ground every so many steps when travelling round the shrines. This exercise was also carried out by secular pilgrims. At the end of each day they would mark the point they had reached, and return to it to resume their progress the following day; the circuit of P'ou-t'o chan might take a month.

At popular festivals there could be large crowds. An account of the temples at Miao-fong at the beginning of this century describes how this shrine, about 40 miles north west of Peking, held its annual festival for a fortnight from the first day of the fourth lunar month:

> From the beginning of the pilgrimage season to the end, day and night, the crowd of pilgrims passes endlessly, and the smoke of the incense rises without interruption. It is a remarkable sight... The pilgrimage roads have grown in number over the course of the years, and no road is so busy as that from the north... carriages and horses crowd the highway and the multitude of fires and lights shine like stars at night. If you count those who come each year by all the different routes, there would probably be a total of hundreds of thousands of people, and if one estimated all the money spent, you would again get a figure of several hundred thousand taels. The quantity of perfume burnt must be greater than anywhere else in the world.

Pilgrims used to bring back paper flowers and hats from Miao-fong and incense ashes which would be added to the brazier on the altar at home; at Mount T'ai and elsewhere the special memento, regarded as a valuable charm, was the impression on paper of a jade seal kept in the temple on the mountain peak. Equally, votive offerings were very common, and tablets recording the answering of prayers were also placed in the temples.

Mount T'ai, as we have seen, enjoyed imperial patronage; but it later became the greatest of all the popular pilgrimage sites, ₑspecially favoured in the first four months of the year. At the foot of T'ai stands T'ai An, 'the city of peace', with the temples dedicated to the spirit of Mount T'ai; and from it, through the Heaven Gate, lies the steep road that leads up the mountain, with massive steps, 10 or 12 feet wide, made of single blocks of stone. Most pilgrims ascended on foot, but those who could not do so were carried in basket chairs: the truly devout ascended on their knees, as on the *Scala Santa* in Rome. The road is paved with stone, and is about five miles in length, with numerous landmarks and temples on the way. In the mid-sixteenth century, two Chinese officials made their way up Mount T'ai, not so much as pilgrims, for they seem to have been of a sceptical turn of mind, but as visitors. Nonetheless, their diary of the visit captures the atmosphere of the place vividly:

'As the moon is very bright and the weather peaceful, let us together ascend T'ai chan, to see the beautiful and wonderful and famous features of this, the Great Mountain'. I promised. Next morning we rode horses abreast out of the rampart and looked north. Fogs and smoke belted the waist of the Mountain. Mr Yeh and Mr Fu accompanied us two miles to White-crane Spring, where the water bubbles out from cracks: in drought it shakes down. A hundred paces to the west is Combing and Washing Tower, now in ruins; no one knows when it was built. Two miles northward is the King's Mother Spring, whose waters are bubbling, never dry: from this pool the villagers use the water when praying for rain.

Fifty paces north by the Cliff of Liu is a statue of that immortal. During the Sung dynasty towers were built here, now there are only ruins and flourishing grasses. As we reached the base of the Mountain the sun rose on the face of the eye out of the clouds: so different is the prospect from near and afar. All peaks stood up. In surprise and admiration we wondered at the stretch of scenery. 'I seem to be satisfied', said Censor Li.

From the foot of the Mountain to Horse-return Ridge is more than ten miles. Between the hills, among the valleys and rocks, the forceful waters splash, rush, fall in cascades in marvellous beauty, sparkle in their course, and are lost in the river. Riding single file, we reach the foot of the ridge, servants had the sign of weariness: we rested and drank tea. Changing into sedan-chairs, we penetrated a deep forest, crossed rocks, between slanting cliffs, with stone steps at danger-points. Here are trees and grasses with a canyon in front, clear water with small green fishes on the surface. A Taoist offered me cakes to feed them, but they went when I flung a stone a them. Walked on the Wan Yin, where the great Chin Shih Huang Ti planted five pine Trees, and when they died men replanted them. These are more than a thousand years old, branches and trunks twisted like green dragons ready to fly away...

We reached South Sky-door, which from a distance looks like a ladder hanging on the Mountain-side. This is a Dangerous Place. Here we changed to small chairs, passed up and through several miles eastward...came to a monastery, where we put on cap and gown to worship the Daughter of the Great Mountain God: every spring people come here from all quarters; if their heart is not sincere, they are punished at once. I heard it, and I know it is true.

On westward several steps toward Tai Ping, Great Peace – this is the highest place on the Mountain. Here is a large rock more than ten feet cube, sharp-edged, brightly coloured. We four sat on the rock and felt tired in the legs. Two of us went on top: marvellous views, sky-climbing peaks, beautiful flowers, grassy cliffs, sounds of animals and birds. Countless mountains and rivers to be pointed at: none in the world can be higher than this. We go about happy, not knowing whether in Mountain or Sky.

Forty steps below Dragon Mouth, down a dangerous path, we went to a cliff over a deep canyon; I lay down my body to look down; my hair stood up. A Taoist tells us that sacrifice-people jump over this cliff, and become fairies... We are ashamed that the Taoists cheat the people and destroy life; we shall ask the Chow official to shut up this path... West of the cliff are five peaks. The sun is over. We can go no farther. So we return to the monastery, drink, and each writes two poems on the wall. Wood-cutters and cow-boys are among the trees like a picture. It was too late to visit the Hall of Li Tai-po.

If Mount T'ai was the place of sacrifices, Nan Yo, the great peak of the south, was the place of prayers and of ancestor worship, where success for the future was sought and thanks for past favours rendered. It was sacred to the fire-god, and was much visited until the early part of this century: the pilgrims had their own songs, and these were issued in the form of a manual, which included the correct prayers and rituals. A curious touch was that pilgrims used to train their hair in imitation of the style shown on images of Buddha, even though they were Taoists; and Buddhists and Taoists shared the Holy Street which led to the mountain top. The main temple was dedicated to the fire-god; by a strange contradiction it contained the Deluge Tablet, a very ancient inscription, dating from before 1100 BC which records how the third Chinese emperor, Yu, overcame a great flood. But this attracted little attention from the pilgrims, whose chief interest was in the ascent of the mountain.

The most spectacular of the Chinese mountain shrines is Mount Hua, the western peak, the most remote of the five, on the headwaters of the Yellow River in the Shansi range. The temple of the west peak is some five miles from the foot of the mountain, and the pilgrim path was a mere footpath, nothing like the stone pathways at Mount T'ai; yet the mountain was studded with shrines and one traveller counted 227 sites which were worthy of attention. One of the attractions for pilgrims was the wealth of stories about holy men, magical beings and ladies of the court who had retired there. It is also the most beautiful of the peaks, 'called Hua because all things blossom here' and in the early 1900s, there were still many hermits, living in artificial caves cut into the rock face, often with terrifying precipices below and approached only by chains fastened to the rock. The last part of the ascent was extremely difficult: at one stage the traveller came to the 'rock of repentance' and many pilgrims turned back because of the fearful climb ahead, where an almost vertical stone ladder was only passable with the aid of chains on either side, and rose nearly a thousand feet up the mountain, followed by a razor-edge traverse called the 'Grasping Pass'. At last the path came to the Golden Palace Temple below the peak itself. Such a site could only be visited in summer, and the priest used to ensure that he had provisions for three years each autumn, in case he was cut off by exceptional weather. The remote nature of the place attracted not only the very devout, but also refugees from civil or political troubles, who found safety in the fastnesses of the mountain.

Tibetan pilgrimage

The difficulties of the ascent of Mount Hua are not unlike the pilgrim routes of Tibet; the hazards of the journey are an essential part of the pilgrimage, and add to the merit gained from undertaking it. The most dramatic of the Tibetan sacred mountains is Mount Kailas, in the western Himalayas, between the sources of the Brahmaputra, Indus and Ganges. It has been argued that Kailas is the original of Mount Meru, the peak at the centre of the world in Buddhist myth, and it is sacred to Hindus, Buddhists and to adherents of the native Tibetan Bon-po religion alike. Only a handful of western travellers have ever succeeded in reaching the region, and it has its place in the history of exploration as well as in the annals of pilgrimage, which indicates its sheer remoteness. The object of the relatively small number of pilgrims who managed to reach Mount Kailas was to make a circuit of the mountain, a distance of some 32 miles. The truly devout performed the exercise of prostrating themselves at full length on the ground every few steps, thus adding to the difficulty and length of their journey, but also to the spiritual merit achieved. On the approaches to the mountain lies Lake

Manasarovar; to encircle this was also part of most Kailas pilgrimages. It was a longer expedition, about twice the length of the circuit of the mountain, but less arduous. On the route around Kailas were five *gompas* or Buddhist monasteries; a further eight stood around the lake, so it was something of a religious centre. For the Buddhists, the mountain is particularly associated with Milarepa, the greatest figure in Tibetan Buddhism at the beginning of the twelfth century. He is said to have gained control of the mountain from the local Bon-po worshippers by a contest of magic with their leader, which began when Milarepa made his circuit or *pradaksina* of the mountain keeping it to the right in Buddhist fashion, while the Bon-po priest kept it to the left, as the old custom demanded.

Kailas is, by all accounts, a remarkable site in a spectacular region, a huge four-square sugar-loaf peak rising from the high plateau, which changes its aspect with each alteration of weather and with each hour of the day, catching the least colour and reflecting it back, appearing or disappearing in snow or cloud. In the last decade, a trickle of Hindu pilgrims have been allowed to perform the pilgrimage, and a number of Tibetans have done so. Most of the *gompas*, destroyed in the Cultural Revolution, have been rebuilt. But Kailas remains a remote fastness, despite the building of roads; it can never have been a place thronged with travellers, and it is always likely to be one of those names to conjure with, a distant and unapproachable idea.

Pilgrims to the mountains of eastern Tibet were more numerous, and the major pilgrimages to the holy mountains of Tsa Ri, Dokerla and Amye Machen took place every twelve years before the Chinese conquest. At Tsa Ri, the ordinary problems of travel in the mountains were complicated by the presence of brigand tribes near the shrine, who made a habit of plundering the pilgrims, even though the latter generally travelled in large groups, often ten or fifteen thousand strong. In the late

16. Mount Kailas, holiest of the Tibetan mountain peaks, with a temple and prayer-flags in the foreground.
(© 1987 Russell Johnson)

nineteenth century, the government at Lhasa would send emissaries to the chiefs of these tribes to negotiate suitable presents, in return for which they would undertake to refrain from attacking the pilgrims. When the chieftains were ready to swear their oath 'a yak was killed with a sword, its heart torn out, and its skin stretched on the ground. Each of the chiefs of the *gting-klo* had to walk on the skin and, having taken the oath, eat a piece of the heart. After the chiefs, all the *gting-klo* warriors – there were usually about a thousand present – walked across the skin one by one and took the oath'.

At Dokerla, on the Chinese-Tibetan border, the pilgrim set out to walk round the mountain, or rather group of peaks; in Tibetan Buddhism, walking round a holy place has particular merit, and monasteries often have special arrangements to enable pilgrims to perform such circumambulations around a particular shrine, making the task difficult by suspending ladders from chains to form the route. Dokerla requires twenty days' march to complete the circuit: it is believed to be the haunt of supernatural beings, in particular the hermit Kha-ba dkar-po, who has lived here for centuries. He communicated with pilgrims through dreams at one of the resting-places, and such dreams were recorded in a precious book kept at the next temple. At Assilaka, the pilgrims climbed a small mountain and left their pilgrim staffs as an ex-voto. The most difficult part of the journey was the pass of Dokerla itself, a narrow rocky ridge of crumbling stone: a French traveller wrote of it that 'nowhere on earth can a road used by men rise so madly against the sky'. In the spring, the really devout pilgrims would venture out onto the slopes of the mountain itself, roped together, to find an inevitable death in its snows; the men of the nearby village of Londjré, when the snows had gone, would search the gullies of the mountain in order to strip the bodies of their silver ornaments. For the true believer, here as at Kailas, the guidebook to the pilgrim route encouraged him to see, not the savagery of ice, snow and rock, an illusion of this unreal world, but a brilliant paradise, a holy place where everything grew in luxuriant profusion, inhabited by heroes and gods.

Because of the inseparable nature of state and religion in Tibet before the Chinese invasion, the capital, Lhasa, was a major pilgrim centre. The festival of the Great Prayer at the Tibetan New Year attracted thousands of pilgrims; it was started in 1409 AD, and had a distinctly learned character, as it was centred on the three great Buddhist teaching monasteries, and was the time when titles were awarded to outstanding students. The Potala itself, the palace of the Dalai Lama, was also a place of pilgrimage, and the statue of Avalokitesvara there was reputed to have shed tears at the time of the Chinese invasion, recalling the many weeping images of medieval Europe. The focal point of the pilgrimage to Lhasa was the Jokhang, the 'cathedral of Tibetan Buddhism'; here the figure of the Buddha brought to Tibet by the Chinese princess who introduced Buddhism in the seventh century was kept. As elsewhere in Tibet, the pilgrim was expected to circumambulate the temple, and there were three forms of this ritual, for the interior, exterior and for the city itself. There were many other lesser sacred sites in Lhasa associated with the history of Tibetan Buddhism and its great figures, just as Rome's sacred sites echo the history of Christianity.

In Japan, pilgrimage dates back to the early days of Buddhism, following in the pattern of Indian and Chinese Buddhism; as elsewhere, it centred on mountains and on temples associated with the great figures of Japanese Buddhism. But just as Taoism took over from Buddhism in China and adopted many of its practices, so in Japan the national religion, Shinto, coexisted with the new cult, and the two were effectively combined for nearly a millenium. It was only with the restoration of the Meiji emperors in 1868 that the two religions were declared to be separate, and in many places Shinto and Buddhist

18. A young pilgrim before a statue of Fudo; an early nineteenth century print by Kuniyoshi. (Private collection)

shrines are to be found on the same site. Pilgrimage was unknown in Shinto before the Buddhist period, though the ancient Shinto centres such as Isé, the temple of the sun-goddess Amaterasu who is the reputed ancestor of the Japanese imperial house, became focal points for pilgrimage. There was less emphasis on pilgrimage as a means of self-improvement than in Buddhist teaching, and the journey seems at times to have become an organised pleasure trip.

For the Japanese Buddhists, the three mountains of Kumano, south of Osaka in central Japan, were a favourite object of pilgrimage from the tenth century onwards, encouraged by imperial patronage. The Shinto *kami* of the three mountains, local deities who represented the forces of nature, were identified as the Bodhisattvas Amida, Kwannon and Yakushi. The roads to the mountains were sometimes so thronged with pilgrims that writers compared them to ants; nonetheless the journey was long and difficult, and we hear of pilgrim-masters or *shi* who were responsible for guiding pilgrims through the mountains to the sanctuaries. Like their Hindu counterparts, they were also responsible for publicising the pilgrimage.

By the fifteenth century, the pilgrimage to the thirty-three shrines of Kwannon, the Bodhisattvas of mercy, was well established as an act of penance; because Kwannon was believed to look down mercifully on the deeds of mankind from a height, the sanctuaries were on mountain-tops. They were dotted across the narrow part of the main island of Japan, Honshu, and the journey was again an arduous one. The pilgrims travelled in white robes, which were marked at each sanctuary they came to, and existed on charity. They sang hymns related to the places they visited, and when they reached the shrines, performed acts of self-denial.

The most famous and extensive of all Japanese pilgrimages is that associated with Kobo Daishi, the founding father of the sect known as 'esoteric' Buddhism, which takes place in the

19. Pilgrims at the Roben waterfall, Oyama from a print by Kuniyoshi. Japanese pilgrimage ranged from the social to the extremely ascetic; this is clearly a cheerful occasion. (Private collection)

20. The austere side of pilgrimage: the priest Nichiren on a winter pilgrimage on the island of Sado, from a print by Kuniyoshi. (Private collection)

Shikoku region west of Osaka. Daishi, like Ennin, travelled to China on official business, and used the occasion to make contact with Chinese Buddhists of the esoteric sect. He became the eighth patriarch of the sect before he returned to Japan. Although the first pilgrims to the Shikoku area are recorded in the century after Daishi's death in 835, it was not until the seventeenth and eighteenth centuries that it really came into prominence.

The full Shikoku pilgrimage is unusual, in that it is circular, and great merit is attached to completing the circle; eighty-eight shrines, numbered by tradition, lie on the route. Today the pilgrim traditions are little changed. The *henro* wears white, and carries both an album which acts as a record of the shrines visited and name-slips, which are left at the altars en route, and given to those who provide alms or *settai*; they are treasured by the recipients as a kind of talisman. The album is stamped and inscribed at each temple, and a devout pilgrim may have many impressions of the same stamp from repeated visits. Between the two clusters of temples at the beginning and end of the route lie forty sites stretched out over a distance of a thousand miles. The image always present in the pilgrim's mind is that of completing the circle, the perfection of a spiritual task. The path leads through cities and villages, but much of it is in mountainous territory, often along the cliffs overlooking the Pacific which lead to Cape Muroto; here Kobo Daishi achieved enlightenment. Further on, at Cape Ashizuri, pilgrim legends tell of monks who set sail from here in search of the paradise of Kwannon, exactly as the Celtic monks of Ireland, on the edge of another great ocean, set out on their *immrama*, surrendering to God's will as they drifted with wind and tide in the hope of reaching an earthly or heavenly paradise.

Other stretches of the road lie through inland mountains, those spectacular peaks familiar from Japanese paintings. On one such pinnacle, rising sharply from the valley floor, Kobo

Daishi is said to have meditated, and the more intrepid pilgrims climb hundreds of feet up the narrow path to the top. The pilgrim way is still marked by special inscribed stones, though much of it is now road rather than footpath, and most pilgrims travel by bus. A few hardy adventurers continue to do it on foot; they can follow the old path, away from the busy roads, though lack of use means that such tracks are increasingly neglected.

Interestingly, these Japanese pilgrimages were an actual example of a 'liminal' rite; anthropologists have classified all pilgrimages as such an activity, but in Japan pilgrimage was undertaken at exactly that adolescent stage when, in primitive tribes, the individual is temporarily ejected from society in order to re-enter it with a new, adult, status. Even the word *henro* was written with characters that implied a journey to distant places or to a frontier; now the conditions of pilgrimage have changed, and the characters have been altered to a more generalised image.

The main Shinto pilgrimage was, and is, the journey to Isé, the chief shrine of Amaterasu, the sun-goddess. Isé is a remote mountain site in the heart of Japan, and the shrine is rebuilt every twenty years on two neighbouring sites in the town. The pilgrimage was less religiously oriented than the Buddhist one, and at times became simply a pleasure trip, much as some western European pilgrimage centres gained a secular reputation. In the eighteenth and nineteenth century, the pilgrimage was sometimes started on impulse, in a kind of religious frenzy: the pilgrim would suddenly abandon his work and home, and set out without money or preparation, relying entirely on alms. At the other extreme to this unpremeditated pilgrimage were the pilgrimages to the mountain peaks at Haguro and Omine, where a harsh discipline was the order of the day. Pilgrims underwent physical ordeals and endurance tests, in an atmosphere designed to emphasise the need to overcome all physical attachments and desires in order to achieve spiritual revelation. This formalised the arduous conditions which all mountain journeys involved, and deliberately made a cult of them, in contrast to the gentler precepts usually invoked on pilgrimages.

CHAPTER SIX

Common ground

S o far, we have looked mainly at the differences between the pilgrimages of the major religions: their different origins and history, the different sacred places at which they worship. Yet behind these historical and physical divisions lies a surprising degree of unity. Some of this arises simply from the definition of pilgrimage itself: for example, all pilgrims are travellers. But there are other, less expected common themes, and it is possible to see pilgrimage as a phenomenon with its own culture, which crosses religious boundaries and produces a common set of practices.

Let us begin with the pilgrims themselves. The earliest records of pilgrimages in any religion are always those of people with high religious or secular rank; this is partly because of the way in which records survive, favouring the highly educated man who could set down his experiences in writing, over the ordinary traveller, who could only tell his own story to his friends, but partly because travel was expensive and difficult; the result was to produce a historical progression in all religions, from pilgrimage as the preserve of the influential or exceptionally determined – a rarity, in fact – to pilgrimage as a mass movement, generated and sustained by the needs of the ordinary believer. The first pilgrims set out either alone or with a personal retinue: Egeria, who travelled from north-west Spain to the Holy Land in the years 381-4, was undoubtedly a lady of means, while after Christianity became the official religion of the Roman Empire the bishops who visited Jerusalem were able to use official transport. Humbler pilgrims could travel relatively easily to Jerusalem, but only because of the admirable road system of the Empire: they were the exception rather than the rule before the fifth century AD. Likewise, in China and Japan, the early Buddhist pilgrims of whom we hear were religious leaders of high rank or exceptional gifts. Even Tripitaka, who set out for India virtually as a fugitive, without official permission, returned nonetheless to an imperial welcome, having travelled most of the way in considerable style. Ennin, seeking out the sacred Chinese sites just as Tripitaka sought out those of India, could only get to China because he was a member of an official embassy from Japan; but when he stayed behind without permission and made pilgrimage, he went as a poor monk, begging his way.

The second stage of development is when we find organised bands of pilgrims from a variety of backgrounds coming together to undertake their journey. If the purpose of pilgrimage was almost always personal and individual, the image of a band of pilgrims is just as familiar as the idea of the pilgrim as a solitary traveller. Most pilgrims, for purely practical reasons, travel in groups: companionship, safety and mutual support all make this necessary. Unpopular pilgrims, such as Margery Kempe with her hysterical outbursts of weeping when she contemplated relics or listened to sermons, could find themselves rejected by their fellows, and would have considerable difficulty in continuing their journey.

In Hinduism and Buddhism, pilgrims in some areas formed associations with wider implications than a single journey to a single shrine. The Mahratta pilgrims at Pandharpur are perhaps the most extreme example; it is said that the men from a particular village will pass along their route at the same time, to the hour, year by year. Their association lasts throughout the year and is a kind of religious grouping centred on the annual ritual. Equally, confraternities for pilgrimage existed in China, where members paid into a common fund for the purpose of their journey, and set out behind a banner proclaiming their place of origin. In Japan, pilgrimages to the national shrine at Isé or to Mount Fuji were organised in a similar way, but the object of the *Isé-ko* and *Fuji-ko* was to send one or two members each year to Isé or Fuji as representatives of the whole group, rather than for all their members to depart together.

In areas where a crossing of the sea or the desert was needed, a system of organisation grew up to meet the demand, usually based on existing merchant traffic: the caravans to Mecca were originally organised by Arab traders, while the Venetians became the agents for the pilgrim trade to Palestine in the fourteenth and fifteenth century. The laws regulating the pilgrim traffic from Venice show how important this business was to both the Senate and the merchants of the city. The would-be traveller, having found a ship on which there was a place, entered into a very precise contract with the captain of the galley, who also acted as a kind of tour operator in Palestine itself. There were two sailing seasons, after Easter and after Ascension Day, which were recognised as the regular departure dates, and pilgrims knew that they could find transport if they arrived at these times. The contract was regulated by the Venetian state, though it was almost impossible to enforce it when it concerned actions many hundreds of miles away on the high seas or in a foreign country. The going rate was around 40-60 gold ducats when Felix Fabbri, a friar from Ulm in Germany, travelled in 1480: this included the voyage to and from Jaffa, all provisions, a good place on the galley, and a fortnight's stay in Palestine, during which time all arrangements were to be made and paid for by the captain. The captain, for his part, was anxious for as swift a voyage as possible, but might also want to do some trading on the side; so the pilgrims tried to prevent him from stopping at strange ports and loading merchandise so that they had less room on board. Equally, he was to depart promptly; otherwise the pilgrims would have to spend more money in the city while they waited.

Felix Fabbri went on one of these Venetian 'tours' twice, in 1480 and 1483, and we have many other accounts which confirm his. They give detailed lists of the baggage and equipment needed, what kind of wine to buy, where to find good water. The galleys were basically merchant ships, working under sail, but with oars as a means of getting in and out of harbours: the sleeping quarters were a large cabin marked out with spaces about one and a half feet apart for each pilgrim. Other than meals, there was little to do on the voyage, as Fabbri notes:

> Some....go about the galley inquiring where the best wine is sold, and there sit down and spend the whole day over their wine. Some sing songs, or pass their time with lutes, flutes, bagpipes, clavichords, zithers and other musical instruments. Some discuss worldly matters, some read books, some pray with beads; some sit still and meditate....some work with their hands, some pass almost the whole time asleep in their berths. Others run up the rigging, others jump, others show their strength by lifting heavy weights or doing other feats.

There were dangers, quite apart from those of storm and tempest. The pilgrims had to keep clear of the sailors as they worked, because the tackle was primitive and heavy: the chief officer was killed by a falling spar. And when they reached Corfu, they were advised that the Turkish fleet was on the warpath; the Venetian authorities recommended that they should turn back. Some of the company did so; but the rest, Fabbri among them, insisted on continuing, and were able to get the captain to agree. They reached the Holy Land safely, but only had nine days in which to see the sights, because the captain was imprisoned for four days and counted this as part of their time, even though the pilgrims could do nothing until he was released. On the voyage back they were delayed by headwinds, and ran out of water, only just reaching land in time, but they arrived at Venice in safety.

Fabbri's fuller description of his second pilgrimage, which he made largely because of the shortness of his stay at Jerusalem on his first visit, fills in a good deal of the details of how the organisation worked. As a more experienced traveller, he inspected two galleys this time, that of Agostino Contarini, with whom he had travelled before, and a newer one belonging to Pietro Landi; the captains vied for his custom, but he chose Landi's as it was more spacious. There was something of a race between the two captains on the voyage out: Contarini won, only to be held up because the local Saracen officials insisted on dealing with both galleys together. For the Saracens too, pilgrimage was a business matter, to be regulated carefully, and it took three days to reach agreement with them. Once they reached Jerusalem, they were in the hands of the prior of the Franciscans there, the 'Father Guardian of Mount Sion', and it was he who organised their excursions, both within and without the city, and their attendance at the services in the Church of the Holy Sepulchre. They were also escorted by two officials whom Felix Fabbri calls 'Calini', who acted as interpreters and guides. They were men of considerable standing, with sufficient authority to deal with the local Arabs who often banded together to bar the pilgrims' way, to pelt them with stones or demand a ransom for allowing them to continue unhindered.

The nearest parallel to the Venetian pilgrim tours was the system of caravans by which pilgrims arrived at Mecca. The most important of these was the *mahmal*, which left Cairo each year bearing the *kiswah*, or new covering for the Ka'bah, as well as a large sum of money for the treasury of the holy cities of Mecca and Medina. As recently as 1932, the departure of the *mahmal* was a major ceremony, with the whole of the garrison of Cairo on parade. The caravan went either by sea from Suez to Jeddah, or overland: the old sea-route, abandoned because of the danger and difficulty of navigating the Red Sea under sail in favour of the land route, and reopened once the steamships came. When the *mahmal* travelled overland, the Egyptian government provided a military escort of three hundred men and two field guns to keep marauding Bedouin tribesmen at bay. The steamers, however, reduced the voyage to a mere three days, and began the opening up of Mecca to the ordinary pilgrim which was completed by the building of the railway from Damascus to Medina in 1908. At Mecca itself, the role of pilgrim guide, which has no permanent equivalent in Christian Jerusalem, belongs to the *mutawwif*, his responsibilities range from the arrangement of lodging to ensuring that the correct rituals are followed, though he has no formal religious standing.

For an example of the organisation of pilgrimage within the religious hierarchy, we have to turn to India. With Hinduism's looser definition of priesthood and the ubiquitous system of hereditary offices, the business of arranging pilgrimages has become a traditional responsibility, and the majority of temples have their *pandas*, who not only look after the pilgrim's needs at the shrine, but positively recruit pilgrims to come to it. They maintain an extensive network of clients, usually from a specific district, who may be encouraged to return again and again over the years; and their children may appear in turn at the shrine, to be looked after by the same family of guides a generation later. Even the most enthusiastic and ambitious medieval clerics in Christian Europe never reached this level of promotional activity; but they had less need of it, because the reputation of a shrine could be spread in other ways. Because the Christian church as a whole was a formidable organisation, there was no need for its officials to recruit and manage pilgrims as a separate, specialist trade.

Most pilgrims would not think consciously about such organisation, unless, like Fabbri in the hands of the Venetian captains and their Saracen counterparts, they were entirely dependent on outsiders. Those who travelled on foot or on horseback in small groups through friendly territory needed no organisation: for them pilgrimage was a carefree mode of existence, and as such it attracted the idle and the curious. A medieval cynic observed that

> He that on pilgrimage goeth ever
> Becometh holy late or never.

Another writer warned that 'the most part [of pilgrims] that cameth, cometh for no devotion at all, but only for good company to babble thitherward, and drinke dronke there, and then dance and reel homeward'.

These cheerful bands could only set out without assistance if they knew that they could find lodging along the way; and pilgrim inns and hostels were a familiar feature throughout western Europe in the Middle Ages. At the end of the pilgrimage, there were often magnificent buildings, the best example being the hostel built by Ferdinand and Isabella, the 'Catholic kings', at Santiago de Compostela. Jerusalem was well equipped with places for visiting pilgrims, even when the local authorities were hostile. Along the route, there was a generally accepted tradition of hospitality towards pilgrims. At Mecca, on the other hand, in a country where tents were a familiar means of accommodation, there was no such tradition, and Sir Richard Burton found that he had to lodge with a family, while a Moslem traveller in 1932 commented: 'It is a remarkable fact that while all Christian churches have established hostelries in Jerusalem...where the poor can find free hospitality for a week, the Mohammedans have no similar institutions in Mecca...' Pilgrim hospices were an ancient tradition in the east: Ennin, journeying to the sacred mountain sanctuaries, notes that there were places along the road at which both monks and laymen could stay free of charge, quite apart from the main Buddhist monasteries, which, as in the medieval west, offered hospitality to royal officials as well as fellow-monks. The hostels were in the wilder parts of the country, away from the main roads used for trade and imperial business, but on the routes to Mount Wu-t'ai. He describes the first such hostel which he saw:

> The people nowadays call it the Shang-fang Common Cloister. For a long time there has been rice and gruel there, and, when men come there, regardless of whether they are clerics or laymen, they are lodged and, if there is any food, it is given to them, and if there is none, none is given. Since neither clerics nor laymen are prevented from coming and lodging there, it is called a common cloister. At the cloister there are two monks, one of whom is pleasant of disposition and the other dour. There is [also] a yellow-haired dog. When it sees a layman, it growls and snaps, with no fear of blows from a stick, but when it sees a monk, whether he be its master or a guest, it wags its tail very submissively.

Thereafter he stayed in a series of hostels or 'Common Cloisters', five in all, each a day's march apart, until he reached the foot of Mount Wu-t'ai itself. In the present century, 'mountain societies' offered support to pilgrims on the road from Peking to Mount T'ai. At roadside stalls, the members dispensed food and drink to pilgrims, and even practical help such as shoe-mending. The societies were supported by donations from would-be pilgrims before they set out, and contributors were given a poster to put up outside their house to say how much they had contributed.

Although word of mouth could spread the news that such hostels existed, pilgrims who had made a dangerous and difficult journey were eager to set down their experiences for the benefit of others; and the earliest travel guidebooks we have are those designed for the use of pilgrims. At their simplest, as in the case of a pilgrim who travelled from Bordeaux to the Holy Land in the fourth century, they are little more than a note of distances between places and the names of the towns along the route. Other later guidebooks concentrate on listing the holy places to be seen. But we quickly meet the pilgrim as tourist as well: the main guidebook to Rome, which was originally written about 1150-75 and continued to appear in printed versions well into the sixteenth century, offered a list of places of interest, a collection of stories about the ancient monuments, and a suggested tour of the city. The earliest version gives a bare list of purely classical remains such as triumphal arches, palaces and other monuments, without any reference to their Christian connections, though the author ends his places of note with an account of 'places where the saints suffered'. The legends are part-Christian, part-pagan. Some are garbled accounts of monuments which survive today, such as the bronze equestrian statue of Marcus Aurelius on the Capitol, known popularly then as the horse of Constantine (though the author denies this, and tells a different story to account for it). Others account for the transfer to Christianity of such sites as Santa Maria in Aracoeli and the Pantheon, and describe the foundation of the three great basilicas.

The guide to Compostela, written in the twelfth century, is much more practical, beginning with lists of the four great roads to Compostela and the stages on the road, but the travellers had to pass through difficult and little-frequented territory, unlike the roads to Rome, which were a well-trodden route. So Aiméry Picaud, the author of the guide, gives thumb-nail sketches of the local conditions. The route from Bordeaux was especially bad, and he gives a direct and vivid account of it which conveys much of the trials and tribulations of pilgrimage, mixed with a good deal of suspicion of foreigners and their ways:

> [On the road from Tours] having crossed a strip of sea and the Garonne, you get into the Bordeaux district, where the wine is excellent. The Saintonge people already speak in a rather uncouth way, but those of Bordeaux are even rougher. Then to cross the Landes of Bordeaux you need three days' walk, because people are already tired.
>
> It is a desolate country where everything is missing. There is

neither bread, nor wine, nor meat, nor fish; no water and no springs; the villages are few and far between in this sandy country, where, however, there is a fair amount of honey and millet; and there are pigs.

If by hazard you cross the Landes in summer, do be careful to protect your face from enormous flies which abound there, and which are called wasps or gadflies; and if you are not careful with your feet you will find yourself almost up to the knees in a sort of marine sand which invades the place.

After having crossed this country you will find yourself in Gascony.

The Gascons are frivolous, talkative, full of mockery, debauched, drunken, greedy, dressed in rags and they have no money; nevertheless, they have been well taught how to fight and are remarkable in their hospitality towards the poor. Sitting round the fire they have the habit of eating without a table, all drinking from the same cup. They eat an enormous amount, they drink wine without it being watered down and are very badly dressed. They have no sense of shame and the master and mistress lie down along with their servants on a pallet of mouldy straw.

Leaving this country, the road to St James crosses two rivers. It is impossible to cross either of them save by boat. And cursed be their boatmen. In fact, although these rivers are quite narrow, these terrible boatmen have the practice of demanding from each person who goes from one side to the other, whether he is rich or poor, a sum of money and for a horse they extort four pieces by force. Now the boat is small; it is only made of a single tree trunk and can hardly take a horse. Not only that, but after having received money the ferrymen take such a large number of pilgrims that the boat upsets and the pilgrims are drowned and then it is that these boatmen are wickedly happy because they take from the dead all their things.

In this region there are a number of bad toll collectors. These people, frankly, should be consigned to the devil. They actually

go in front of the pilgrims with two or three sticks to extort from
them by force unjust fees, and if any traveller refuses to give in
to their demands and give them money they hit them with their
sticks and take away from them their taxes; and greatly swearing
they even rummage into their trousers.

In the Basque country, the road to St James crosses a
noteworthy mountain called the pass of Cize, first because it is
the entry pass into Spain and here also important commodities
are transported from one country to another. To cross over there
are eight miles to ascend and then eight miles to descend.

Then, descending from the top of the pass, comes the country
of Navarre. These people wear clothes which are black and short
and which end at the knees in the mode of the Scots; they wear
shoes which they call *lavarcas*, made of untanned leather with
the hairs of the beast still on them, which they attach to their feet
with thongs, but which only cover the soles of their feet leaving
the upper part bare. They wear wool cloaks of a dark colour
which come down as far as the elbow. These people are badly
dressed and they eat and drink badly; with the people of Navarre
the entire household, servant and master, maid and mistress, all
eat from the same cauldron in which all the food has been
thrown. They eat with their hands without using spoons and all
drink from the same goblet. When one watches them eating one
is reminded of dogs or pigs gulping gluttonously; and listening
to them talk sounds like dogs barking.

A Buddhist guidebook for pilgrims to the Chinese sacred
mountains, the *Guide for obtaining audience at the four famous
mountains*, is in many ways a sharp contrast to the sheer
practicality of Aiméry Picaud, who might be describing any
journey through strange territories. The instructions for reaching
the holy mountains are the second, and least important, part of
the book, and the emphasis is on spiritual guidance, the
pilgrim's attitudes and state of mind, as well as his conduct on
the way. He must obey four precepts: respect the sacred
writings, look on all living beings with love and compassion,

keep his mind free of evil thoughts, and concentrate his spiritual attention on the Buddha. He is warned that there will be dangers and difficulties along the way, but he should regard these as mere dreams or illusions. On the other hand, he should not make his difficulties worse by lack of foresight, and should find a master or guide if possible, whom he can follow; he should choose his companions with care; and he should enquire as to the correct route for the next day, so that he does not get lost and become disheartened. He should not try to hurry, but should adapt to circumstances, and stay as long or as short a time in any place along the way as may be necessary. The pilgrim should respect the customs of monasteries where he lodges; if the monks are strict in their observances, he should follow suit, but he should not criticise if they are lax. Laymen should pay generously for their lodging; monks, on the other hand, who are put up free of charge, should not be angry if they are turned away. Above all, the pilgrims should never lose his temper or self-control; pilgrimage is a journey in search of the truth, and anger or impatience can lead the pilgrim away from what he is seeking.

Very similar advice is to be found in the guide distributed at Temple One of the Shikoku pilgrimage in Japan: in both cases, much of the advice is a restatement of Buddhist teaching, mixed with thoroughly practical advice. As the Japanese guide puts it:

> A hasty journey with a heart full of business does not lead to piety. One is only brought to shame by it. Without other intention or thought, calmly and without haste, with 'Namu Daishi Honejo Kongo' [the pilgrim prayer] upon one's lips – that is how to make the true pilgrimage.

Most of the early books on pilgrimage in the west are simply guides or records of the details which later travellers might need to reach their intended destination. But in the east, partly because the distances involved were greater and partly because the journeys made by pilgrims were not necessarily on a well-defined route, we have autobiographies rather than guidebooks. Fa-Hsien's record of his travels in India is admittedly fairly brief and descriptive, but he is concerned with the physical state of the shrines and of Buddhism as a religious force in India; while Hsuan-Tsang or Tripitaka is really writing an account of a personal spiritual quest, perhaps the first example of this kind of narrative. The dangers and hardships of the journey are part of his spiritual development, rather than a hazard that might prevent him from reaching his goal. Ibn Jubayr's travels culminate in his visits to Mecca and Medina, but, like Tripitaka, he spends a good deal of time visiting teachers and holy men on the way there. The Buddhist pilgrims also differed from their western counterparts in that their journeys were searches for written materials as well as spiritual benefits. For a western pilgrim, Moslem or Christian, arrival at the shrine was the ultimate objective, and thereafter nothing mattered. For the Buddhist traveller, the return home was equally important, so that the valuable texts and images gathered on the journey could reinforce the teaching of the faith at home. Just as Fa-Hsien and Tripitaka sought such materials in India for Chinese Buddhists, so Ennin acquired authoritative books in China for the faithful in Japan. These were a kind of missionary journey in reverse, there are parallels for it in early Christian pilgrimages to Palestine, when the fathers of the church sought to make contact with the sources of Christian tradition in Palestine, both written and oral.

In the fifteenth century, we begin to find accounts of Christian pilgrimages which go beyond the sphere of mere guidebooks, though the latter continued to be produced. When William Wey, fellow of Eton College, went to Jerusalem in 1458, the record he made of his travels included rates of exchange, lists of practical details, a travellers' phrasebook for Greek and Hebrew, and a note of place-names with their shrines and the indulgences attached to each of them, all keyed in to a map. There are, it is true, two accounts of the actual pilgrimage, but when the author of the earliest English printed guidebook came to use Wey's work in preparing his own text, it was the practical notes which he kept. Similarly, when Felix Fabbri and his companions set out in 1483, one of them, Bernhard von Breytenbach, wrote a guide which was illustrated, when it came to be printed at Mainz in 1486, with woodcuts of six of the great cities along the route, based on pictures by an artist whom Bernhard had brought on the journey for that purpose, and many other illustrations.

Felix Fabbri, however, is more typical of his age: his book does not aim to serve as a manual, and indeed he has considerable doubts as to whether pilgrims ought to be encouraged to set out for Jerusalem. In a memorable passage, he questions the value of the display of religious enthusiasm he had seen at Jerusalem:

> Good and simple Christians believe that if they were at the places where the Lord Jesus wrought the work of our redemption, they would derive much devotion from them; but I say to these men of a truth that meditation about these places, and listening to descriptions of them, is more efficacious than the actual seeing and kissing of them. Unless a pilgrim hath before his eyes some loving example of devotion, the place helps him little in the matter of true holiness. Those weepings and sobbings which are common at the holy places arise for the most part from the fact that when one pilgrim weeps another cannot refrain from tears, and so sometimes all of them lament together; or because some people have the art of working themselves up to weep even in matters unconnected with religion. Such people as these shed many futile tears at the holy places, and make a howling at almost all of them, not because of the power which the place exercises over them, albeit the places do certainly tend to devotion, but because of the ease with which they weep. But I have no doubt of this, that were there ten good Christians in my cell at Ulm, who had a desire to see the Holy Land and the places sacred to the Lord Jesus, I could rouse their devotion and stir up their souls more deeply by my talk about those places than if

they were actually lying bowed to the earth in the holy places themselves.

Fabbri is unusual in that he gives a full account of his homeward journey, and regards his pilgrimage as ending with his return to Venice; he is also a remarkable writer, full of shrewd observations, who recreates not only the broad outlines of his journey, but seems to want to depict all its details. He was writing specifically for his fellow-monks back home at Ulm in Germany, and tells us that he took notes as he went; so his book is almost a diary, written day by day. In many ways, the diary kept by Ennin of his pilgrimage in China eight centuries earlier is similarly detailed, and designed for the same kind of audience. What we are witnessing is no longer a devotional exercise, but the emergence of modern travel writing: there are relatively few 'travellers' tales' in either book, but they are all the more compelling for their down-to-earth interests.

But these writer-pilgrims are a select company, a mere handful out of the millions. How can we distinguish the ordinary pilgrim as he sets out on his journey? Whether in Europe or Japan, the adoption of special dress is one of the constant features of pilgrimage, ranging from a badge to a ritual preparation of both person and clothing. The Japanese pilgrims on their initiatory pilgrimage wore white, carried a staff, and rang a bell as they went; Chinese pilgrims might coil their hair in imitation of the style shown on Buddha's image and don an apron bearing characters which said where they were going; Hindu pilgrims put on saffron robes, and like their Moslem counterparts, took temporary vows of asceticism: we have already looked at the preparations for the *hajj*. The medieval Christian pilgrim might adopt 'a staff, a *sclavein* and a scrip', as a London preacher recommended in 1406. The staff was a sensible accessory for any long journey on foot, a weapon as well as an aid to walking, while the *sclavein* was a tunic made of coarse cloth which came down to below the knee. The scrip was a pouch in which the pilgrim kept all his goods and money. To this was often added a large broad-brimmed hat with a scarf attached, which provided some protection againt sun, wind and rain. Sometimes these items would be blessed at a special ceremony, but this was never an established ritual like the Moslem preparations for the *hajj*, with its specific prayers. The most distinctive mark of Christian pilgrims was usually worn on the way home, a token showing where he had been, such as a palm, brought back from Jerusalem; from this, pilgrims were often called 'palmers' in medieval England. Travellers to Compostela used to sew cockle-shells to their garments; these shells would have been very distinctive away from the Atlantic coast. Such tokens were replaced by lead badges in the twelfth century; each shrine had its own symbol, and the ardent pilgrim might have dozens of them, often sewn to his hat-brim. They were regarded as good luck tokens, a kind of minor equivalent of a relic. Chinese pilgrims earlier this century would wear a little red hair ornament in the shape of a bat to show that they had successfully completed a pilgrimage.

Pilgrim costume set its wearer apart from the rest of society and proclaimed his mission. It emphasised that he or she was no ordinary traveller, but someone whose ordinary role in society was suspended for the time being. It also offered privileges, freedom from the tolls and taxes levied on merchants and others who travelled on business, and the right to lodging and food which was often – but by no means always – regarded as the pilgrim's due. This right was most widely recognised in Christian Europe; in the east, it seems that the early Buddhist travellers expected to have to pay substantial sums in the course of their wanderings; Ennin took gold and other goods with him to China, but even so ended his journeys in poverty, like other pilgrims. Tripitaka, after a fortunate encounter with the ruler of a Buddhist kingdom bordering on China, was given an escort and a generous contribution in gold and kind in order to continue on his way. Pilgrims from Europe to Palestine paid, as we have seen, large sums for the voyage from Venice to Palestine and back, and only at Jerusalem itself could they expect hospitality. And everywhere, a pilgrim who could afford to do so would offer gifts in return for hospitality. The pilgrim was often privileged in other ways. Christian pilgrims in some countries were exempt from civil actions against them or their property while they were away, but their rights were never as wide-ranging as those offered to crusaders. But the returning pilgrim's usual reward, in secular terms, was enhanced status and respect for the journey he had made.

When the pilgrim reached his destination, the rites he performed at the shrine obviously varied widely, according to his religion. Yet there are a surprising number of common features; what ancient ideas or feelings underlie these is beyond our present scope, but their existence is undeniable. The pilgrim at Mecca walks round the Ka'bah in a prescribed direction, and this is a central part of the ceremony. A Hindu pilgrim will similarly perform *pradaksina*, the circling of a shrine, and the same ritual is found in Buddhist Tibet, though here the pilgrim may do so on his knees or stretching out full length at every step. Pilgrims in the Christian churches of western Europe would often process round the shrine, and the distinctive layout of churches on the pilgrimage route to Compostela is due to the need to make space for this ritual: a wide ambulatory extends round the east end of the church behind the altar.

Pilgrims everywhere leave evidence of the fulfilment of their vows, and the *ex votos* or mementoes at a Taoist shrine in China, a Shinto temple in Japan or a Christian one in France may not be so very different: tablets with names on, models in wax of parts of the body cured by prayers, miniature ships recording safe deliverance from shipwreck. One of the most famous collections of such *ex votos* was at St Léonard de Noblat near Périgueux in France: he was the patron saint of prisoners, and those who had escaped from imprisonment or attributed their release to his intervention would make a pilgrimage there and hang their chains by the altar; there were apparently also various instruments of torture which former prisoners had brought. The *ex voto* elsewhere could be a memento of the pilgrimage itself: at Assilaka in Tibet, the pilgrim usually left his staff behind. The practice of leaving a strip of clothing or rag is found at Indian shrines, at the tombs of Moslem saints in north Africa, and was once common in Europe, where it only survives in Ireland and Scotland, at a few 'holy wells'. In China, *ex votos* are equally common, plaster dolls or cardboard cut-outs being the usual form, and commemorative tablets are put up to mark the answering of a prayer. The custom of leaving a written or printed note as a record is also widespread. Jewish pilgrims at the Wailing Wall will slip a piece of paper into the cracks between the stones, while Japanese pilgrims on the Shikoku roads will offer their name-slips to passers-by who give them alms, and will tie prayer-slips to the branches of trees at temples.

The sight of the goal of a long and arduous journey would often move pilgrims to ecstatic or uncontrolled acts of devotion. Felix Fabbri gives an excellent account of what happened at Jerusalem:

> O my brother! hadst thou been with me in that court at that hour, thou wouldst have seen such plenteous tears, such bitter heartfelt groans, such sweet wailings, such deep sighs, such true sorrow, such sobs from the inmost breast, such peaceful and gladsome silence, that hadst thou a heart of stone it must have melted, and thou wouldst have burst into a flood of tears together with the weeping pilgrims. I saw there some pilgrims lying powerless on the ground, forsaken by their strength, and as it were forgetful of their own being by reason of their excessive feeling of devotion. Others I saw who wandered hither and thither from one corner to another, beating their breasts, as though they were driven by an evil spirit. Some knelt on the earth

with their bare knees, and prayed with tears, holding their arms out in the form of a cross...

The ecstatic weeping was well-known among the mystics of the period, and is described by writers such as Julian of Norwich and Margery Kempe. It is unfamiliar to westerners today, because of our emphasis on reason and a distrust of excessive emotion: but Hinduism has a similar expressive tradition, which appears at its most spectacular in the fakirs, with their extraordinary physical feats. Moslem tradition, except in some of the eccentric sects like the dervishes, has tended towards a restrained approach to devotions at the shrines. The restrictions on expressions of respect at the sites in Medina associated with the Prophet are an example. The modern Christian pilgrim is more likely to be impressed by the peacefulness of a great shrine, and displays such as those described by Fabbri would today be discouraged, just as Margery Kempe was frowned on by her neighbours for her behaviour in her local church.

The ultimate type of ritual devotion, unthinkable to the Christian or Moslem, is of course literal self-sacrifice. Although the famous story of devotees hurling themselves under the wheels of the triumphal car at Jagannath has been discredited, pilgrim suicide is recorded from Tibet, at Dokerla, where the 'pious madmen' went out onto the snows roped together until they fell into a crevasse. In India, ancient records speak of suicide in the Ganges at Prayaga and Kashi, and other texts refer both to suicide by fire or by throwing oneself off a cliff, particularly in the Himalayas. This custom was found in China as well: several of the mountain shrines had cliffs specially named for this purpose. Later generations, however, took a dim view of the practices, and under the Ming dynasty a wall was built along 'Throw-body precipice' on Mount T'ai, and precautions were taken to prevent suicides.

Assistant Magistrate Chang, in charge of the district, reported that in one month three people had committed suicide, and he feared a contagion of suicide; so he built a fence-wall across the path. The wall was 300 feet long and 15 feet high. He also hired watchmen day and night. If people came there and lingered, or tried to leap over the wall the guard would inquire about their cases, explain and comfort them, and send them back.

Since then for about 5 years there has not been a case of throwing the body over...Still, afraid the wall might decay, be broken or fall down, and that the watchman might become idle or neglectful, and that later men might not follow this idea and purpose, therefore he asked me to make this inscription on stone to show later people.

When the pilgrims returned home, they could expect to enjoy an enhanced reputation for having made the pilgrimage; something of the special status they had enjoyed during the journey would remain. That status had been in part a purely practical one – as pilgrims they were exempt from ordinary laws which might have hindered their journeys, and were entitled to hospitality where they might not otherwise have found it. But they also had something of a special aura: in Japan the pilgrim was believed to be able to cure illnesses because of his status as a holy figure, and the name-slips he gave were, at the least, good luck charms. In Islam, the title of *hajji*, for one who has made the pilgrimage to Mecca, is still valued, though it is obviously much commoner in these days of mass travel than it used to be.

We have looked at where pilgrims went, how they reached their goals, and what they did once they reached them; so our final question must be 'Why did they go?' Whatever the wider social function of pilgrimage in the eyes of the anthropologists, as a liminal rite, the decision to go on pilgrimage was always an intensely personal and usually highly individual one. There are examples of mass enthusiasm for pilgrimage, but these are few and far between: the gatherings at Wilsnack in 1475 and 1486 were largely crowds of children, and there are no instances of adult pilgrimages beginning in this way in Christian lands, unless the popular movement which accompanied the First Crusade can be called a pilgrimage. In parallel to the official armies, organised by the great lords with the church's official blessing, an untidy mob, led by Peter the Hermit, made its way across Europe, and actually reached Byzantium before the main body of crusaders, only to be slaughtered by the Turks in the Anatolian hills. Even at those pilgrimage sites where the object of reverence was an 'unofficial' or political saint, there was no mass movement, but rather a steady stream of individuals. And although vast crowds may gather at a festival or a particularly auspicious occasion, it is a concourse of individuals towards one given point. The journey is made alone, or in small groups; only at journey's end do the pilgrims come together.

The genuine reasons for going on pilgrimage can be broadly divided into two groups: those who went out of religious devotion, and those who went in pursuit of a solution to a secular problem. The majority of pilgrimages probably fall into the second group. The pilgrim has a request to be put to the deity, a prayer that needs an answer; we have seen the variety of problems put to a medieval European saint or to a modern Indian god. If we include expiation of past misdeeds in this group, as well as visits to oracles in an attempt to resolve future difficulties, it does indeed cover much of the ordinary business of pilgrims. There were also plenty of pilgrims who went from curiosity or a love of travel, and they too need to be included as a third group. The purest form of pilgrimage is that undertaken as a spiritual journey; but even such a pilgrimage must have a physical target, and we have seen how this gave rise to the archetypal pilgrimages, journeys to the places where the founders of the great religions lived. The list of the archetypal sites is a brief one: Jerusalem, Mecca, Bodh Gaya. These included places in the surrounding region, and were always major journeys, to be undertaken once in a lifetime; and since this was clearly impossible for all but a handful of believers, lesser shrines were created as focal points for the new religions. We can see this most clearly in Asoka's reputed distribution of the relics of the Buddha from the original ten *stupas* to eighty-four thousand *stupas*: his action was closely linked to the promotion of the idea of pilgrimage as an act of religious devotion. A similar proliferation of relics provided Christianity with its pattern of pilgrimage centres and it is possible to draw parallels between the activities of Constantine and his successors and those of Asoka in officially encouraging pilgrimage, while in Hindu belief, the gods themselves created or revealed the images to be worshipped. Only Islam, with its rejection of image and relic alike, did not spread its net in this way, though the tombs of the imams provided a number of new focal points.

Belief in the merits or otherwise of pilgrimage as a spiritual exercise is of course the crucial factor in determining how popular it is as an act of devotion. For the Moslem, there can be no question: the *hajj* is prescribed by the Koran, and it is something in which not only those who are convinced believers participate, but also many ordinary Moslems for whom the faith is more a matter of observance than a focal point of enthusiasm. But this is true of most religious rituals; and only in Islam is pilgrimage a specifically prescribed ritual. Hinduism comes closest to this, in that the *tirthayatra* is commended in the Hindu scriptures, and it insists in the same way as Islam on purity of mind and deed as an essential element, a mental rather than practical approach. Very few modern surveys of the reasons for pilgrimage have been carried out; and the best examples come from the Hindu temples in India, partly because of recent interviews, but also because of the records kept by the priests. At Tirumala-Tirapati in Andhra Pradesh in 1980-1, a third of the pilgrims came to pay ritual respects to the god; 12% came for ceremonies such as marriage; and about half came either to request a favour or to give thanks for a prayer answered. At Bakreshwar, a smaller rural temple in West Bengal, the proportions were different; ritual respects of different kinds accounted for almost half the visits, and only one in six were concerned with specific prayers, usually for success in examinations or for resolution of family problems.

The gaining of spiritual merit is associated with most pilgrimages. It is an integral part of the *hajj*, and the Hindu books emphasise that a *tirthayatra* can be one of the means to salvation. But the Hindus also see the merit gained as something which can be used to solve secular problems, and the combination of pilgrimage and prayer is regarded as particularly effective. The system of indulgences found in medieval Europe, and which still survives in Roman Catholic doctrine, works in reverse: a visit to a shrine, which is a material and physical action, can confer future spiritual benefit in the form of an indulgence, or remission of penance for sins not yet committed; in medieval belief, an indulgence could release souls from purgatory. This was too literal an interpretation for the reformers of the sixteenth century, and the abuse of indulgences was one of the reasons why pilgrimages were condemned by them and found little or no place in Protestant religion.

The pilgrims who begin their journeys to seek a solution to a physical or secular problem, or to redeem a vow made in a time of stress or peril, are also concerned with the spiritual, but in a different way, and their quest is a fitting end to a book about pilgrimage. We have looked at it as an institution, as part of the great religions of the world, at its practical implications and surprisingly similar customs; but the essential element of all pilgrimage has so far been touched on obliquely. For pilgrimage is in a sense not only a journey through this world, in physical space, but also a journey out of it, away from the mundane into the realms of the spirit. The humble Indian farmer who walks to a nearby temple to pray for good crops and the Christian mystic who experiences the transcendent at Jerusalem have this in common: they are both acknowledging the presence of, and trying to communicate with, a power which is not of this world. And precisely this may be why men and women have felt the need to go on pilgrimage: surrounded by the petty cares of everyday life, it is impossible to hope for miracles or to find spiritual release. Pilgrimage is liminal not only because it takes man out of his setting in society and places him temporarily outside it; it is also liminal because it takes him out of this world and puts him in touch with the world beyond. The seekers for miracles at Lourdes, the devotees of the Virgin at Knock, the faithful at Mecca, the throngs gathered at the Kumbha mela festival and the Buddhist wanderer seeking self-knowledge have all suspended their ordinary lives to seek out a spiritual goal; and in that they are truly pilgrims in a common cause.

Select bibliography

Beal, Samuel (tr.), *Si-yu-ki: Buddhist Records of the Western World* (London 1884)

Bey, S. Spiro, *The Moslem Pilgrimage* (Alexandria 1932)

Chélini, Jean, and Branthomme, Henry, *Histoire des pèlerinages non chrétiens* (Paris 1987)

Ennin *Ennin's Diary: the Record of a Pilgrimage to China in search of the Law* tr. E.O.Reischauer (New York 1955)

Geil, William Edgar, *The Sacred 5 of China* (London 1926)

Howard, Donald R., *Writers and Pilgrims: Medieval Pilgrimage Narratives and their Posterity* (Berkeley 1980)

Jubayr, Ibn, *The Travels of Ibn Jubayr* tr. R.J.C.Broadhurst (London 1952)

Layton, T.A., *The Way of St James, or the Pilgrims' Road to Santiago* (London 1976)

Maklan, Jka (ed.), *Dimensions of Pilgrimage* (New Delhi 1987)

Morinis, E.A., *Pilgrimage in the Hindu Tradition: A Case Study of West Bengal (Delhi 1984)*

Nolan, Mary Lee, and Nolan, Sidney, *Christian Pilgrimage in Modern Western Europe* (Chapel Hill & London 1989)

Prescott, H.F.M., *Jerusalem Journey: Pilgrimage to the Holy Land in the Fifteenth Century* (London 1954)

Sachou, Edward C., *Alberuni's India* (London 1888)

Snelling, John,   *The Sacred Mountain: Travellers and Pilgrims at Mount Kailas* (London and the Hague 1983)

Sources orientales III   *Les pèlerinages* (Paris 1960)

Statler, Oliver,   *Japanese Pilgrimage* (London 1984)

Turner, Victor, and Turner, Edith,   *Image and Pilgrimage in Christian Cultures* (Oxford 1978)

Vidyarthi, L.P.,   *The Sacred Complex of Kashi* (Delhi 1979)

Vidyarthi, L.P.,   *The Sacred Complex in Hindu Gaya* (London 1961)

Waley, Arthur,   *The Real Tripitaka* (London 1952)

Welch, Holmes,   *The Practice of Chinese Buddhism* (Cambridge, Mass. 1967)

Sources of quotations

p.10   Philo of Alexandria, *The Special Laws*, in *Works*, I, Loeb Classical Library (London 1929) p.139

p.25   Ousama ibn Mounkidh, *The Autobiography of Ousama* tr. G.R. Potter (London 1929) p.176

p.28   Frederika Bremer, *Travels in the Holy Land* quoted in *The Image of Jerusalem* ed. Miron Grindea, *Adam* XXXIII, (Rochester, N.Y., 1968) pp.186-7

p.33   *The Travels of Ibn Jubayr* tr. R.J.C. Broadhurst (London 1952) p.85

p.36   Ibid., p.89

p.57   Jean Froissart, *Chronicles of England, France, Spain...* tr. Thomas Johnes (London 1839) II p.172

p.59   Edward Gibbon, *The Decline and Fall of the Roman Empire* ed. J.B. Bury (London 1913) III pp.225-6

p.106   Fa-Hsien in *Si-yu-ki: Buddhist Records of the Western World* tr. Samuel Beal (London 1884) p.xxxiv

p.118   Sources orientales III, *Les pèlerinages* (Paris 1960) pp.318-9 (author's translation)

p.119   William Edgar Geil, *The Sacred 5 of China* (London 1926) pp.51-3

p.135   H.F.M. Prescott, *Jerusalem Journey* (London 1954) p.60

p.139   *Ennin's Diary* tr. E.O. Reischauer (New York 1955) p.211

p.140   T.A. Layton, *The Way of St James* (London 1976) pp.203-4

p.143   Oliver Statler, *Japanese Pilgrimage* (London 1984) p.182

p.145   Donald R. Howard *Writers and Pilgrims* (Berkeley 1980) p.44

p.146   Ibid., p.43

p.151   William Edgar Geil, *The Sacred 5 of China* (London 1926) p.110